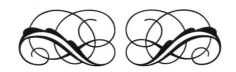

DANCING
With Broken
BONES

A GUIDE TO **LIFE'S CHALLENGES**

Dr. Jasmin Scniark

740 West Locust Street
York, PA 17402

Phone: (717) 854-2547
Fax: (717) 854-0485

International Standard Book Number: 978-1-4675-2780-4

Library of Congress Catalogue Card Number:
Available Upon Request

Printed in the United States of America

Trademarks
All terms mentioned in this book that are known to be or are suspected of being trademarks or service marks have been appropriately capitalized. Use of a term in this book should not be regarded as affecting the validity of any trademark or service mark.

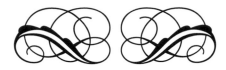

This book is dedicated to the woman who taught me
how to dance with broken bones:

My Beloved Mother
Nell Wiltshire
Born May 16, 1922 – Died August 6, 1982

To my adopted parents
Frank and Janet Shepard

And to my dance partner for the last ten years
Shiloh Baptist Church, York, PA

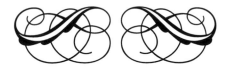

Table of Contents

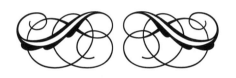

 What others are saying about
Dancing With Broken Bones.

Dr. Jazz writes from the heart, honestly and with conviction. Her advice is mired in faith, knowledge, and valuable real-life experiences - and will truly resonate with a generation looking for guidance and acceptance in a challenging world. This book is a must-read for the faithful looking to improve their position in life and with God.

Dr. Jasmin Sculark is a respected figure throughout the African-American preaching and church community. As her Pastor, I have been privileged to survey her growth from a staff minister to a pastor and preacher of noble rank. Her gifts are many as she shares the Gospel of Jesus Christ with evident passion and power.

When one comprehends "her story" one can readily see why her ministry is so gripping and profound. This native of Trinidad is an inspiration to all who sit beneath the gravitas of her proclamation. How fortunate we are to have captured now in print the spirit of this little lady whose voice and heart are magnanimous! Read these leaves and emerge with a greater determination for Christian witness and service!

Dr. Charles E. Booth, Pastor
Mt. Olivet Baptist Church
Columbus, OH

Every person in pursuit of a dynamic and fulfilling life will be challenged by obstacles, setbacks and even tragedy. In this provocative work, Dr. Jasmin "Jazz" Sculark empowers all of us to persevere in the face of challenges, step off the sidelines of resignation and enter the "dance floor" of life again. This book is a powerful reminder of the capacity that God has put within each of us to "dance," even if our bones have been broken. The music is playing, the floor is open, this work gives us the nudge we need to get into the middle of the floor with God as our partner.

Dr. Lance D. Watson, Senior Pastor
The Saint Paul's Baptist Church
Richmond, Virginia

I am unapologetically a big fan of the preaching of
Dr. Jasmin W. Sculark. She is without question
one of the most enlightening, informative and
inspirational pulpiteers on the homiletical horizon
today. "Dancing with Broken Bones" is her electrifying
sermonizing on the printed page. With the same
excitement, enthusiasm and insight that informs her
powerful and penetrating sermons her writing grabs
the reader by all five senses, from the prologue and
refuses to let them go until the very last page. And
like her preaching, the words of the book will
resonate with mind, body and spirit long after you
have finished reading. Tackling the painful issues of
pain and brokenness; fear and rejection; anger and
pain, Dr. Jazz shows us how and then challenges us
to get on the dance floor and dance into a new and
brighter destiny. "Dancing with Broken Bones" prods,
pushes and even pulls the reader towards a new and
brighter future. Warning: Read with EXTREME
anticipation.

Carolyn Ann Knight
The Seminary Without Walls
Atlanta and Miami

PROLOGUE

Dancing with Broken Bones
A Guide to Living with the Good and the Bad in this Life

How many of us wake in the morning, feeling that we know our body and soul inside out? We have our coffee or tea - we watch the news - we stand on our porch with the autumn leaves falling around us or the birds singing in the springtime - and we think: This is my life. This is familiar. This is what I know and who I am. We feel the familiar floorboards on the porch with our toes – we breathe the same air we breathe everyday – and we start the day with a routine that stabilizes us, readies us for our challenges and responsibilities. And this is good. This is true …. that word again – familiar.

Or is it?

Can we become too familiar? Can we rest too long? Can we get too comfortable with this sense of "self"? Certainly it is grand to know who we are. It is empowering to have our day under control. And … it is even rejuvenating to have a routine that energizes and prepares us for the day, the week, the month – even the year, to come. Can we get stuck, however? With the "good" that we feel everyday – maybe a steady job, a good breakfast, a loving family – can we also live with some pain of which we can't let go? Can we live with a sense that we cannot do something because it has ALWAYS been part of our existence? Maybe we dropped out of college. Maybe we feel that we let someone abuse us. Maybe we have part of a past that does not make us proud. Maybe we hide it all. And…. we live with it. We tell ourselves everyday, subconsciously, that we might have a great family now, but if they knew what we did as teenagers, they might not love us. We might know how to make a nice meal now, but at one time, we didn't have any sense of responsibility, and we let life – drugs, depression, economic situation, or other people – keep us down.

In this way, we have to learn to live with it all – to dance with the good and the bad – to embrace all that is us – and to realize that our story continues, and…. as we turn new pages and start new chapters, life changes and grows and evolves. Above all, God loves us through all of it. ALL of it. We need to know that, and we need to accept it. Also above all, we need to understand our role in all of this. How do we empower ourselves to dance with all our broken bones – all our pain – all our strength – all that others may interpret as "baggage"?

In truth, none of this is baggage. Any path that we have chosen – any injustice we may have weathered – any triumph we may have enjoyed… they are all part of us. Everything we experience, and everything we do becomes who we are. And, none of it changes in any way how God feels about us. It shouldn't change how others feel about us. And, certainly, it should not change how we feel about ourselves.

Exploration of "self" can be a daunting task. It CAN be scary – particularly if you feel that you have done something wrong or chosen a path, which leads you astray for some time. Sometimes, we even feel like we'll never be forgiven for the things we've done– by others, by God, and by ourselves. We feel ostracized, outcast, and broken. What we don't often realize is that the path back to love and acceptance – back to forgiveness and freedom from shame – is all up to us. We don't realize that we have the strength and the fortitude with the help of the Lord to pull ourselves straight and move forward. At times, we don't even realize that, once we've pulled ourselves straight with God's help, we can be accepted for our whole selves by others, and we can rejoin society whole and without secrets or fear. After all, learning from our experiences and teaching others is far more valuable than hiding or running from who we are – what we used to be and what we've become.

> *In this way, we have to learn to live with it all –*
> *to dance with the good and the bad.*

Good people are allowed to make mistakes. Even the faithful can lapse now and then. And, beyond lapsing, even the faithful will tell you that their lapses have helped them. Sometimes the most informed people are those who have been through the most. Other times, the leaders and innovators are people who just have an inherent calm about them – an aura of help and security. It takes all kinds, but what we all need to remind ourselves of now and then is that we are allowed to make mistakes – we are allowed to experiment with happiness – and we are allowed to fall again and again. It is how we pick ourselves up, move forward, and learn to dance with all our scars and pain that measure and communicate the worth of the person.

In picking up and moving forward, we will often feel like hesitating;
we may even feel like not moving forward at all. After all, just like our
morning cup of tea and our familiar pathway to work that we discussed
earlier, we want to stay the course – hold steady and not rock the boat.
But – in life – we need to challenge ourselves to rise and be our best self.
Similar to when we dance, as we grow and embrace new opportunities,
we will experience a bit of a learning curve. We will feel overwhelmed
and may need to alter our perception a bit to accept the benefits that
come from sweat, long hours, and hard work. We will falter as we learn,
and, most importantly, we will eventually learn to move and groove to
our own life's rhythm. We will feel, with body and soul, what is good
for us and what works for us. Taking on new ventures – going back to
school, rekindling with an estranged family member, even giving back and
helping to rehabilitate those in need – is a noble thing. And…. what we'll
be able to do is dance - even if that means dancing with broken bones.

Come dance with me –
Dr. Jazz

UNIT I

Unshackled from Fear:

A Lesson in Confidence from a Leader

Psalms 27: 1-14

One of the most deadly enemies to the people of God regarding faith, security, and love is the spirit of fear. Noted here, in this examination of these concepts, is the fact that we say "spirit of fear" because fear and rejection are just spirits – specters that haunt our lives for no reason. Or – perhaps there is a reason for fear, but…. should we let such an abstract and damaging concept linger in our lives indefinitely? Should we allow such a shallow and fleeting feeling to direct our lives? So many times, I am confronted by people who simply radiate fear. They may seem put together and on top of the world in many cases – secure in a big job or happy to be living in the neighborhood they grew up in – even happy to be free of a bad relationship or a recent bout with financial distress. Why, then, do they not seek a personal relationship outside of work? Why do they resist leaving their familiar surroundings for the promise of something new? Why don't they seek a new friendship or spouse? Why do they still label themselves a financial failure instead of learning from past mistakes? Fear. It is all fear.

We know that "fear" is but a spirit because in 2 Timothy 1:7, we are told: "For God has not given us the spirit of fear, but of power, of love and a sound mind." In our daily lives, we know that fear, simply defined, is dread, uneasiness or anxiousness. Fear is nervousness; fear is dismay, despondence, intimidation, and restlessness. Well-known national minister and non-profit leader in ministry work, Joyce Meyer, says that, "fear is false evidence appearing real." In that way, fear is destructive. Fear, rather than empowering you, paralyzes you. Instead of giving you wisdom, fear causes you to make poor decisions. Instead of strengthening you, fear weakens you. Instead of encouraging you, fear keeps you depressed. Instead of helping you, fear hinders you. And, instead of bringing you success, fear brings you a direct line to failure.

Why, then, do we spend so much time on fear? What is it in human nature that keeps us fixated on such a damaging phenomenon? And, above all, why do we not recognize how false most of the fear in our lives can be? In truth, many of us would be so much further down the road than we are right now – further along in our families, our churches and as individuals – if we had not been shackled by the spirit of fear. And, what is it that we fear? Certainly, it runs the gamut from fear of commitment to fear of success and / or failure. Fear can affect anyone at any time.

In my own life and profession, I see fear in all forms. For example, many young people come to me, unhappy and unfulfilled, feeling that no one understands them. I can see that they are ready for love – ready for families; they should be married, but they are afraid to trust anybody with their hopes and dreams for a future as a wife and mother or a husband and father. Many intellectual people cross my path – all people who could own their own businesses or start a new venture of some kind, but they are afraid to step out on faith – to cross beyond that familiar that we alluded to earlier. I see, daily, people who compromise their own creature comforts – basic needs that would make them happy; they should own their own homes, for example, but don't want to leave their parents' homes or take on more responsibility than a small apartment. And so many people have embarked on the path to education only to undermine their own success and drop out of high school or college before they've even given themselves a chance to work. These are all attainable hopes and dreams, all of which are dashed and cast aside in the looming shadow of fear.

It is quite nearly tragic that so many people see that dream within reach. They have the fortitude, imagination, and intelligence to grasp for it – dream it – even begin to approach it, but…. they allow fear to creep in and destroy their progress. Many times, it is because they're stuck – trapped in the familiar – whether that is the comfort of a mother's home or a family's neighborhood or under the weight of an illness, an addiction, or a crime. Do potential academics from working class families feel that they don't come from "college people"? Do grown people feel that they will be judged for acts committed as teenagers? Do children feel that they cannot fly on their own and, instead, must rely on their parents to help them put food on the table and money in their wallets? The truth is that all of us need to realize our potential and cast aside those fears. We all must learn to dance to the beat of our own drummers – to find our talents – to live with our strengths AND our shortcomings – and to excel and dream beyond what we have traditionally felt were our limits. Yes – that house is comfy. True – maybe you did drop out of school once, but… does any of that mean that you shouldn't try to venture out on your own? Does it mean that you can't try school again? Buy your own house? Dream about a job that no one else in your family has? Or build on what your family has built and expand your horizon a bit? No. The only limits you have are those that you create.

Further, many people remain trapped in problematic or troubling relationships and situations because of fear. How many of us should be confronting friends or family members who are dead wrong – on a path to sure destruction – and yet we say nothing for fear of losing their friendship or loyalty? How many mentally or physically abusive relationships continue because people are afraid of being alone? These are terrible situations and all of them avoidable. Cast out that fear – dance with your strengths – learn to grow and expand beyond those constraints that others place on you.

One lesson that should remain a constant in our lives is that God loves us unconditionally.

On a very personal level, many of us don't even notice how we hold back and exhibit fear. Are we simply afraid to paint our living rooms a bold orange and, instead, keep it beige? Do we forget to proudly display our likes and dislikes – our heritage – our history in our paintings, our photos, our cooking, and our clothing? Do we let this attitude creep into other areas of our lives and create blockades to adventure and enlightenment? How many of us don't travel or see the world because of a basic fear of flying? How many of us don't learn another language because we're afraid of being ridiculed. We need to get excited about our strengths, and we need to learn to dance with our past – to accept our faults, our mistakes, and to learn from them.

One lesson that should remain a constant in our lives is that God loves us unconditionally. Why, then, do we find ourselves even afraid to get excited about God and what God is doing with, for example, our churches, our places of worship? We all want that excitement in our weekly or daily worship yet that old fear of change – loss of the familiar – creeps in. Aren't we ever curious about what God has in store for us and our respective churches? What does He have for us on the horizon? Of course we're curious – even want this change, this love, and this forward motion like our lives depend on it, yet we resist. So many people in my church and in others like it need prayers; they need the love and the warmth of the community and the healing powers of the faithful. They need to be at the altar receiving prayer, and they need God, but they are, ironically, afraid of God and what He might do. They are afraid of change in their lives, and they are afraid of being judged; therefore, they are resistant to healing hands being laid upon them, and they are adverse to the gifts of the spirit. It is interesting to note that, while the spirit of fear reigns so supreme in our lives, the spirit of love, change, and forgiveness has trouble in being asked to dance with the most faithful of our communities. We all need to be free in our spirits and free to let God have His way in our lives. We know this, but we still remain scared of what people will think if we make a leap of faith, shout to the heavens about our strengths, or dance with our problems, laying them all out for God to see – for all to learn from – and for the spirit to heal.

The Bible, in general, speaks of 13 types of fear, all from which God is able to unshackle us:

- The first one is the fear of man. There are 35 references in the Bible to the fear of man. Proverbs 29:25 is one of them. It said that, "The fear of man bringeth a snare: but whosoever puts his trust in the Lord shall be safe."
- The second one is the fear of death (Genesis 21:17)
- Third, the fear of the future (Genesis 46:3)
- Fourth, the fear of danger (Exodus 14:13)
- Fifth, the fear of idol gods (2 Kings 17:35-38)
- Sixth, the fear of dreams (Job 4:15-16)
- Seventh, the fear of evil (Proverbs 1:33)
- Eighth, the fear of war (Psalms 27:3)
- Ninth, the fear of imaginative fears (Psalms 53:5)
- Tenth, the fear of enemies (Psalms 18:6)
- Eleventh, the fear of punishment (Proverbs 1:26)
- Twelfth, the fear of darkness (Genesis 15:12)
- And thirteenth, the fear of ghosts (Matthew 14:26)

Now, these are all negative fears. These are all justifiable, set in stone, understandable fears. There is that one fear that we discussed briefly, however, and that is the fear of God. The fear of the Lord and His judgment is real. It is necessary, and it is palatable, but it is strong and ever-present, and, in many ways, I say we can make it work for us, never against us. So, this healthy fear of the Lord. Where do we find it? In Proverbs 1:7, it says that, "The fear of the Lord is the beginning of knowledge, but fools despise wisdom and instruction." In this instance, the word "fear" carries a meaning of high respect, reverence, piety, in awe; it implies truly standing in astonishment. This is a fear that brings about – as I said earlier – not destruction but, rather, construction; it works for us, not against us. In today's world, too many of us fear the weak and misguided man who can kill the body but who can never kill the soul; at the same time, we do not fear God in this healthy way. God holds our soul eternal and, yet, we don't fear Him in the right way. The Bible says that a man or a woman who does not fear God is a fool. To speak against God and God's will, His presence, and all that He has made is to place yourself as a fool. The worst fool is not the fool who does not believe there is a God; the worst fool is the fool who doesn't know that he or she is a fool! The Bible calls this type of person a "scorner", or a person who mocks God and all that is good. The Bible tells us what to do with that kind of fool; it says that we are not to answer a fool for then we, too, will be fools in the same way. Now, do we want to seek out being a fool? Or... do we want to strive to understand what makes this particular fear a good one, a healthy one, and the one true fear that will lead us to the right path. Throw away all those earthly fears – all those that hold us back – and embrace this reverence for your God. In this way, you stand no chance of being that fool.

In our biblical text, Psalms 27, we are introduced to David, who is the second King of Israel who refused to be shackled by fear. In fact, King David sticks in all of our minds as a leader, as one who shows no fear – ever – only his reverence and respect for God (that healthy fear about which we talked). As David establishes himself as Israel's King, one of the things he has to deal with is that, with every elevation, with every door that is opened, there comes greater opposition and resentment – the "haters" emerge, and envy and jealousy prevail. Has anyone noticed that the more the Lord blesses and opens doors for us, the greater it appears the opposition and the stronger the resentment become? In this case, David ought to be enjoying the fruits of his labor and the blessings God has bestowed upon him and yet, at the same time, he has to deal with the Sum of All Fear. David not only has to deal with the inner fear of failing, but he ends up having to deal with a fear that begins to surround him.

Now, how can we learn from David? What should we notice that David used to become unshackled from fear? In our biblical text we see four things that helped David: his confidence, his concern, his cry, and his courage. Let's examine each of them and see how we can apply them to our own personal and professional lives.

David's Confidence

First, we see David's confidence. David starts off this text not with fear but, rather, with faith and confidence in God. He says, "The Lord is my light and my salvation whom shall I fear? The Lord is the strength of my life, of whom shall I be afraid?" (verse 1 and 2) In this verse, David expresses great confidence in the Lord. The reason he can have such confidence in the Lord in the midst of fear is because the Lord has become his light and his salvation. Salvation, here, can be translated as a stronghold. David is saying that the Lord has become his stronghold, a fortified place, and, thus, no one can harm him. Light signifies understanding, joy and life, and the stronghold or salvation signifies defense. Sometimes the child of God has to take a defensive stand, yet there are times when the child of God – in this case, David – has to take an offensive stand by shining light or understanding onto the enemies of God. Because the enemies of God operate in the darkness, the Bible says clearly that these people and their deeds are evil, away from the light – and joy and life.

David goes on to establish who God is to him—that He is not only his light, but He is his life. Beyond salvation, God is his strength. "When God is my light and life, my stronghold and my strength fear and being afraid has to disappear." This clearly illustrates David's confidence in God – that God is his light and life, his stronghold and his strength.

With David knowing his position in Christ, he raises a rhetorical question, a question that does not need an answer. He asks that with God being both his defense and his offense, whom shall he fear? And we know the answer is no one. Standing on the fact that there is no one that he needs to fear but God, David is able to take an offensive stand and sheds light on his enemies. How many of us know that it is just a matter of time before all people will expose what is in their hearts to others? The Bible says, "Fret not yourselves over evil doers for they shall soon be cut down, and do not be envious against the workers of iniquity for they shall soon be cut down like the grass and wither as the green herbs" (Psalms 37:1). God will shed light on our enemies; He will let them say things and behave in certain ways so that we will sooner or later know who they are. It is impossible for darkness and light to be in the same room. And as David reminds us, "when the light comes, the enemies of God will have to flee" (Psalms 27). David is clear in his analysis that when God sheds light on our enemies, then there is no fear. Fear functions in darkness, but when light comes–light which represents my faith – fear has to go. Apart from God being those things to David, David would have fainted in the midst of fear, which is no different than any of us.

David's Concern

In this stage, David muses that he really has good reasons to fear and be afraid. As he says, "For I am surrounded by the sum of all fear. I am surrounded by trouble". David's concern isn't regarding God, necessarily, but rather regarding other people. Remember, we discussed the fact that, often, when someone is met with favor from others or even God, the critics gather – the masses oppose the positive. Those who oppose David seek to keep him shackled by fear, something not uncommon for all of us in modern day, so we can empathize.

The first group David mentions is the wicked (verse 2) "When the wicked come up against me". Who are the wicked? By definition, "the wicked" or a "wicked person" is an evildoer or someone who is seeking to cause harm, ill will or injuries with the intent to hurt or break another person. David specifically says the "wicked" in a very general way, a fact that suggests that the "wicked" involves people, in general – people who probably don't even know about you or David, for that matter. These people are inherently opposed to you – wicked in their own ways – impervious to others. In most cases, those who experience "the wicked" have not necessarily done anything to them; in fact, the "wicked" will oppose you no matter what. They don't care for yours or David's thoughts and concerns; they only seek to destroy and create issues. They are evil. Nothing they do or say is personal; they don't care if you're married – they don't care what church you attend – they just exist to stand in your way like they tried to stand in David's way. We can all handle the wicked. If we can handle one of them and their one-dimensional, predictable ways, then we can handle two – six – twenty – one hundred – thousands. The "wicked" do not stand as your enemy; they don't move against you like a foe. They may try to harm you, but they are transparent, and, with fortitude of faith and the lack of fear required to face them, they are powerless.

Wicked people are weak people. As we have established, they are uninformed and not in touch with a single person. They are unhappy and bent on harming for the sake of harming – not to further a cause – not to stop a movement – just to be mean – to manifest their evil ways. And, wicked people need to travel in packs. As we all know, when we feel evil, ill will, or harm meant to come our way, it comes in groups – at least in twos. Bullies – minions of the wicked – do not like to fight alone; they need support for they have no fortitude – only fear.

It is hard to face a group of naysayers, though, isn't it? It is hard to stand up to the wicked – to your adversaries – your bullies with no purpose. What do you do? What do you say? What did David do? In reading the account of David and his adversaries and foes, we find that they were, at one time, his friends. Now, this is hard to swallow. His friends? What do you do when your friends become your foes? How do you face that? Beyond bullies and wicked people, we – and David – now have to deal with back stabbers – naysayers who say one thing to our face and another when we turn our backs. What hurts most for David is that, publicly, these are his greatest supporters – yet, privately, they are his greatest enemies. And, we've all been there, haven't we? And, we know, firsthand, that it takes true strength and lack of fear to overcome this atrocity – this betrayal. And, we know how the story starts and ends, don't we? Once we gain success, once we have all the support, or once we show promise, the naysayers and enemies come back. Now, the bullies we didn't worry about, but these people.... these people are tricky; they can go both ways – either turn on you in times of need or in times of power. And, David experienced this too. All of a sudden, after he achieves success and begins to truly lead Israel, the greatest supporters become "David haters." This suggests that they were enemies, foes and adversaries all along, doesn't it? They were just pretending to be David's friends and supporters. So – should we all be careful? When we overcome our Goliath – on pure faith and lack of fear – should we watch our backs? Should we watch for the haters – those joiners who will topple you every chance they get? Yes. And the way we do that is to conquer fear – maintain faith – and restore our love for God and ourselves. That's what David did, and he overcame his Goliath AND his enemies. Successes we know bring out the best and the worst in people, and we have to be ready – free of fear – spirited and ready to grow and move forward.

David experienced this from a whole host of people – a large company of like-minded individuals, in this case bent on bringing him down. As is the case with all bullies, they have to act as a group, again…. fearing and loathing the worst in themselves, they have to use the group dynamic to reassure themselves of their rocky hold on what they feel is right. In the text, we find David surrounded by them, having been laid siege by the worst – all afraid to attack alone. In this time of need, when those who oppose him are warring against him, David feels forsaken and left alone. This is a concern, isn't it? We do need to note, however, that he doesn't let it stop him. He notes it, concerned and ready to defend himself, and he moves on. In this heightened state, David can move to his next strategy – noticing the false testimony of others, a valuable trait to have for any of us brave enough to forge our own paths in life.

Now, in David's case, the enemy goes to an extra high by establishing false witnesses who rise up to give false testimony or speak against David and others, despite knowing very little of the truth. Again, this is something we can all relate to. And, really, while in our intelligent minds, we know not to listen to these people or, by contrast, not give any credence to what they say or do, instead we let them hurt us, and we worry what others will think. And David, in his day, he knew that this was one of the most dangerous groups of people that he would have to face down. This group would truly test his faith. This is one of the most dangerous groups in all the people that David has to face. David says that they breathe out cruelty, violence, false testimony, and injustice. This group is dangerous because they will prey on the lamb, the weak sheep. This group does not care who gets hurt in the process as long as they have an audience in which to release their poison. They are what the Bible says in the book of James, "Their mouths are filled with deadly poison. And it spread like wild fire among the defenseless." (James 1:8) They are despicable people, all of whom we may know too well. After all, the goal of the false witness who breeds out cruelty is to cause doubt among the sheep – the flock, the devoted, hard-working followers of the chaste and faithful. These people rarely pick on someone their own size; instead, they are like wolves, preying on those who they know they can intimidate and hurt. David knew this, and he knew that they would never approach anyone directly but they would indirectly attempt to spread their poison. We all know these people, and we can overcome these people.

In our modern day, we experience people who hide behind the guise of "freedom of speech" to hurt and confuse the masses or to spread falsehoods and stereotypes among hard-working people. Do we, in truth, let these people off the hook? No. We call them out in the media and in our public forums, and we make them accountable. As members of a society who can do that, we need to remember that, in fact, we CAN overcome – like David. I recall, many times in my own pastorate, that I had to face those types of people. They hid behind a building, and their love for the building, but they could not stand me. In fact, what's funny is that they could not stand each other, but the one thing they had in common was that they could not stand me. They used their position in the lives of the seniors in the congregation to lead everyone astray. All I could do was what David did next: I learned to cry out to God. I encourage all of you to take note of this lesson.

David's Cry

In the midst of all of this, David cries out to God (verse 7) saying, "Hear, O Lord, my cry with my voice. Have mercy also upon me and answer me. When thou say seek ye my face, my heart said unto thee, thy face will I seek." In this cry, David shares his biggest fear, which is that he does not want God to forsake him or leave him. He is crying out asking God not to leave him, not to forsake him. And the reason why David has this concern or fear is because people had forsaken him in the past, so why, in his mind, would God be any different? We've all felt this. We've had people leave us, not support us, even ridicule us or ostracize us for our mistakes AND for our successes. Poor David – everyone from his father and even his mentor, Saul, who was once his friend – has forsaken him, even turned on him. David thinks and makes the mistake that we all make everyday; we sometimes lapse and believe that God will leave us. In our darkest hours, when we succumb to temptation – when we've been hurt or felt that we hurt another, we feel abandoned. Maybe we feel that we deserve to be abandoned and left to our own devices, but... still, we ask for forgiveness, we ask for support, and we beg – as David did – praying to be left in God's good graces, fulfilled, helped, and, above all, NOT left alone. This is hard for us to see, isn't it? That God will not leave us; He will not forsake us. No matter what we do.

Now, I ask this often, but... how many of us do feel that our lapses in judgment will condemn us to a life devoid of human contact AND forsaken by God? God is not a man, but we treat Him like the weak mortals who do forsake us. Why? Because our fellow man condemns us? Because we feel ill will from our neighbors? Because we have known the pain of standing up to someone we love with terrible consequences? Yes. Absolutely.

Have we stolen? Did we hurt someone unintentionally? Intentionally? Have we been lazy? Did we allow another to be forsaken? Have we committed a crime? Did we fall into addiction? Did our marriage fail? Have we lost contact with a child – a parent – a friend in need? All of this troubles us. It all hurts us and others. It even hurts God. But will he forsake us? Never.

As we examine David and his plight – and ultimate triumph, it is easy to see his progression. It is not as easy to see our own. I see, many times, young people who have come to me, lost and confused. Maybe they've dropped out of school – maybe they've come from a failed marriage – maybe they're trying to put an adolescent prison sentence behind them. They all share one thing in common – a sense that they are not worthy of love and that they will not be forgiven. They seem to think that society will forsake them –that they are not capable of moving on or becoming a better version of themselves. We can recall the beginning of the book when we discussed familiarity and a certain comfort level with the good and the bad in life. To be clear, I mean a complacent sense of the familiar, one that has frozen us in a perennial state of denial or inaction as opposed to a fulfilled, "I've embraced all that is me" comfort level. I find these young people in that state, wanting to be at another level of comfort – one in which they dance with the good and the bad – where they accept what they've done in life – terrible things and fantastic things – as God does.

Let me share with you my biggest fear after my own divorce. I had many concerns. Where would I live? What would I do? What would everybody think? I had moved from Washington, DC to Columbus, Ohio. I had not made my own friends yet, having come from somewhere else. I only had experience living on campus at college, with some church friends, and then with my husband. I had never lived on my own before; I had never taken care of myself. I remember being nervous, uptight, overly concerned about the next day – and the day after – all my tomorrows, really. One minute it seemed I was in school working on my masters, happily married, and all was calm in my universe then…. the world, as I knew it, had come to an end. And at one of my lowest points, Pastor Jenkins and his wife, called me. They had been trying to help my husband and I reconnect and reconcile, and when I heard their voices on the phone, I just felt so ashamed and upset; after all, the marriage had failed anyway, and I didn't know how I appeared to them anymore.

Pastor John Jenkins of First Baptist Church of Glenarden and his wife, Trina Jenkins, invited me to their home, and I stayed for a couple of days. After dinner in the evenings, we began to talk well into the wee hours of the night about this divorce and my fears about my life moving forward. After two days of sharing my fears regarding not being able to pick up the pieces and move forward, I said to him, "Pastor, do you know what I am afraid of the most?" I said, "I am afraid I have disappointed God because this marriage ended. I am afraid that He would walk away from me just like my father did, my mother did by dying, and my husband did just recently." I said, "It's just a matter of time and I know God will too. He'll take His gifts and His anointing from me because I failed Him." And that truly was my biggest fear – that I would miss God's purpose for my life. My destiny, it appeared, was to have God abandon me like everyone else by walking out of my life. I mean, it felt like it had been that easy for people to do. I wasn't sure what I had done wrong, but I knew I would pay for it – for my failures. And for some of us, that's our greatest fear – that nothing we do is good enough, that we fail often, and that everyone will leave us – and, rightly so – after all, we haven't earned support and respect, have we? So we try so hard to earn God's approval. We work hard at it. We can't stand the thought that God may abandon us. One of the reasons we are like this is because the church has taught us for so long that if we don't do right, live right, and cross all of our "t"s and dot all of our "i"s, that God will turn His back on us.

On that night, Pastor Jenkins, shared a bit of scripture with me that has since liberated me from the fear of God turning his back on me and not wanting to use me anymore. On that night, he shared a scripture that broke the shackle of fear that God would take back all of the gifts he had given me and that I so loved – preaching and teaching His Word. This bit of pivotal scripture is found in Romans 11:29 and it reads, "For the gifts and the calling of God are irrevocable." Your Bible may say, "The gifts and the calling of God are without repentance."

Repentance. What a concept. Repentance means a change of mind. And, here, in this verse that changed my life and my perspective, Paul is saying that when God calls you and gifts you, He does not change His mind. Man has a change of heart and a change of mind but not God. There is nothing you and I can do to make God change His mind from loving us, gifting us, and calling us. If He called you in 2002, He called you in 2003. If He called you and gifted you in 2005, then He called you and gifted you in 2006. If He used you and anointed you in 2010, then it's the same call in 2011. And the same call and gift in the years to come. This means that there is nothing you and I can do that will cause God to change His mind, reverse the calling and gifts He bestowed upon our lives. Even if you are locked up in prison, God still has a calling upon your life. Having a child out of wedlock did not change God's mind about loving, calling, and gifting you. Having an abortion did not change God's mind about calling and using you. Having an affair did not change God's mind about using you. Doing or selling drugs did not change God's mind about using you. Dropping out of school did not change God's mind in any way. Being raped did not change God's mind about loving you. Cutting yourself did not change God's mind about using you. Losing your temper did not change God's mind about using you. Lying on your income tax form did not change God's mind. There was nothing that you did in the first place for Him to use you; He loved you and trusted you unconditionally, knowing what gifts you had and what service you were capable of executing. Leaving the church did not change His mind. Nothing did. Nothing will. It is called unmerited favor. The gift and the calling of God are without repentance. He said to Jeremiah, "Before I formed thee I knew thee; and while you were in your mother's womb, I called you to be a prophet" (Jeremiah 1:5).

Now, because we are gifted people – and people of considerable use to God, we do need to change our lives – to work through our issues, change for the better, and not repeat the mistakes that we've made. We will not be condemned for trying and failing or even for lapsing in judgment. Instead, God may use us even more, knowing that we have new gifts and new knowledge to use to help others. So… cast out your own fears; you don't need anyone to do it for you. Become the person you know you can be – the person God has always known you could be.

David's Courage

This brings me to David's courage. We see his confidence, his concerns, his cry and now his courage. And that's what it is going to take to break the shackle of fear. It is going to take courage. First it is going to take courage to believe God. Anyone can doubt God but people with courage can believe God. David said, "I would have fainted by now but I had the courage to believe that I would see the goodness of the Lord in the land of the living." (Psalms 27:13) I had the courage to believe that while I am here that I would see God's goodness. It takes courage to admit your fears.

And it's going to take courage to wait on God. To wait means to trust in him. Remember, fear is false evidence appearing real but, "Faith is the substance of things hoped for the evidence of things not yet seen." (Hebrews 11:1) You are going to have courage to admit your fears; trust God with those fears. Stand firm in the truth. And you are going to need courage to live in the present, not in the past or the future. Someone said that courage is not in the absence of fear but courage is in the midst of fear. It's facing your fears with courage. It is getting on that plane, taking that cruise. It is going back to school, attempting to make that relationship work. It is walking out of a relationship that is abusive and unhealthy. It takes courage for a man or woman to admit their wrongs and share their struggles and weaknesses.

In 2002, the Shiloh Baptist Church of York, PA, took a step of courage, by calling me to be their pastor. No Baptist church in the city of York, PA – before 2002 – would ever consider calling or electing a woman to be the pastor of a church. In spite of the opposition from within as well as outside the church, Shiloh broke free from the shackles of fear and elected me to be their eighth pastor, the first female to be elected to serve as the senior pastor of a Baptist church, and the first woman to be called to pastor a church in the city of York, PA ever.

From that moment on, God has been asking us to dance with courage and not fear. In the nine years since, we have had some good things happen without our courage as well as some bad things; however, we have kept on dancing. In fact, we have enjoyed many blessings after being unshackled by that fear; in the nine years since Shiloh took this bold step, we ordained women to be Deacons of our church; we have purchased a new building and moved our congregation from the south side of the city to the west, another step in this new journey of courage.

It will take courage to dance with those broken bones – those good and bad things that life – that God – sends our way.

To Dance with Confidence and Courage: An Epilogue to Unit One

I tell the story of David often, and I realize that most of my members are familiar with David's story. I see in their eyes the fact that David has been both a literal and metaphorical example of courage to them growing up in the church. I hear in their voices the conviction and confidence they have when they reference David and his dramatic story of Goliath. I do not, however, sense that many of them – until they've read with me, talked with me, and, yes, danced with me – have truly taken the story to heart and lived a life that exhibits courage and confidence in every way.

Now, I can't teach people how to implement such life-changing qualities into lives lived for years without them. I can't teach people the absolute value of such life force values if they won't listen or, further, don't sincerely want and need such movement and change in their lives. I can, however, live by example and tell people countless stories of how those down on their luck, stuck in a rut – whatever way you want to put it – have overcome and moved on to lives lived in God's favor and with tremendous daily earthly joy. I can talk to you endlessly about people living God-fearing and happy, productive lives who saw more in themselves and also moved to a higher plane of enlightenment – simply by making little daily changes that altered perception and, therefore, outcome of certain situations. I can recount the many people

I've met who have lived with past secrets and issues that they felt they could not move beyond or even talk about and, yet, they do with fantastic results regarding living lives in service to God, to others, and to themselves.

As we move forward in this book, I hope that the Biblical account, my stories, and my words will inspire you to create your own dramatic and personal path to God and to a life lived to its fullest. As I reflect on the many people I've met and counseled in my life, I can see them all clearly: The single mother with an adequate job who listened to friends and family over the years and began to feel that she had been forgotten – left behind by a man – could only hope to get by and provide for her kids. That same single mother who went back to school and worked on herself to make sure that, not only were her kids provided for, but that she had a life and career that she loved – and she could enjoy both spiritual and material growth and wealth that, previously, she would not have envisioned. I think of the young man who came to me, confused, in trouble with his peers – with his neighborhood – with the law. That same young man showed such intelligence and promise that I watched with pride, as he danced with his issues and partnered with those restless qualities that had him so misguided and in trouble, turning them, instead, into entrepreneurial spirit and new life – business, relationship, and more.

It amazes me daily to see all those dancers – all those people embracing their lives – their pasts, their faults, their strengths, and their suddenly brighter futures. I always know that they have it in them, and I always let them steer those qualities toward their own path. It is my hope that listening to inspiration in this book – and reading between the lines – and taking all the stories to heart – and recognizing the need for further improvement and positive movement in your own lives – will impact this amazing generation of readers, churchgoers, and Godly people to help others, improve their surroundings, and to elevate themselves. I pray that you all will get happy feet, and that you will dance – and even if, for whatever reason, you stopped dancing – that you will find the courage to dance again.

What are your hopes and dreams? What makes you happy on a daily basis? For some, that happiness comes from simply living with and loving their families. For others, they may want their own businesses – they may want to run for public office – they may, simply, just want to finish something they've started or hoped for but never accomplished – a degree, a weight loss, a new home, and more. You might not understand the neighbor committed to growing and managing her own organic farm or the member of your church who wants to travel to a new country four times a year, but maybe you can understand creating warmth and love in your own home by cooking for your family or listening when they talk. You might be able to understand simply getting your finances in order so that you can afford a new car or have the means to try a new restaurant, buy your grandchildren some books that you remember as a child, or take those steps to change jobs, start a side business, or take more days off work.

Our lives are not necessarily our own, but we are the stewards of them.

Our lives are not necessarily our own, but we are the stewards of them. We decide what we do and how we do it. God empowers us with whatever we need to live a rich life and is there to oversee our plans and bless us when the time is right. Of course, He'll challenge us too, and He'll send us what He thinks we need in life. We need to be prepared for that, and, again, we need to embrace what He sends us and what we do with it. Dance with yourself – all your faults and all your strengths. Be brave and confident enough to stand up and actually say what you want to see happen. Sometimes, admitting to yourself that you feel shame or fear is the first step towards overcoming obstacles or becoming role models yourselves in your respective communities. So…. open your mind and prepare to be inspired and moved. This book can help give you that final boost towards your life's goals.

Your assignment as we just scratch the surface of our topics here is to begin taking stock of your life. Effortless and something that is easy to become second nature as we move forward, I want you to write in this space all those things, good and bad, that you feel you need to learn to "dance" with – a bad credit score, an extreme talent in cooking, a loving family, a job you don't like – again, good and bad – list it here. As we move through the book, gradually, you won't have to write it down anymore, these thoughts and goals will become second nature.

_____

_____

_____

_____

_____

_____

_____

In Psalms 51:8, David said "Make me to hear joy and gladness; that the bones which thou hast broken may rejoice". This text has been one of my life texts. It has helped me throughout my childhood and adulthood to dance with broken bones – whether that broken bone came from the abandonment of my father or the early death of my mother when I was only fourteen years of age. I had to learn to dance with those broken bones. Or whether it was the broken/failed marriage after only four years that helped me to learn to dance with those broken bones. Whether it was from the rejection that I felt from many in ministry for many years….. I've had to dance with all those broken bones. Even the brokenness of friendship; I've had to learn to dance with that pain as well.

God blessed me and invited me to join Him on the dance floor, and just when I was getting comfortable dancing by myself with my brokenness, God selected a partner for me to dance with. This has been my dance partner for the last ten years, which is the Shiloh Baptist Church in York, PA, and they also had their own broken bones.

Suddenly, we were both on the dance floor learning to dance with our broken bones.

Over these past ten years and – really – throughout my entire life, I've been learning to dance with the broken bones of fear, rejection, forgiveness, and I've been seeking to find strength to live with my brokenness.

I found strength to remain on the dance floor in spite of all of my brokenness, and I did this through my faith, which is founded in my relationship with God and God's word. I trust that these biblical texts, as well as my own personal reflections, with help you do the same.

I look forward to seeing you on the dance floor with all of your broken bones.

UNIT II

Unshackled from Rejection:

Redemption for the "Outcasts"

Genesis 21:1-21

If I were to take a poll at any given time by a show of hands, in any of my sermons, presentations, or speeches, I'm sure I would not be the only one who has ever felt the pain of rejection. While no one wants to experience rejection, we all have experienced it in some form at some point in our lives. Whether we have memories of exclusion on the playground or currently feel the old "alone in a crowd" conundrum as adults, we have felt it or been a part of it in some way.

There is an old nursery rhyme called, Little Sally Walker (Anonymous, American Nursery Rhyme / Folklore). As many nursery rhymes find their origin in truth and coping, this one is no different. And, it is interesting to note a couple of things: One, that it is universal and popular, and two, that it addresses issues of exclusion, favoritism, belonging in a crowd, and voyeurism. Such mores and odd values are so embedded in society that, it appears, it is not unusual for these qualities to be transferred to a child's nursery room and, therefore, brought to playgrounds and other benign, presumably happy play situations during which children are learning from one another. Disturbing, to say the least. Regardless, the nursery rhyme goes something like this: "Little Sally Walker sitting in a saucer, rise, Sally, rise; wipe your weeping eyes. Put your hands on your hip, and let your backbone slip. Oh, shake it to the east, shake it to the west, and shake it to the one that you love the best." And if you were in another neighborhood, there was a second verse, "Your mama said so. Your papa said so." The implications are universal – whether you've heard it before or are hearing it for the first time, – it is upsetting. Sally Walker, a child, sad and sitting apart from everyone else – in her saucer. And, as I said earlier, we accept this nursery rhyme, we sing it out, we laugh, and we never wonder who may relate to it on a different level – a level replete with loneliness. Why was Little Sally Walker depressed or down? Why was Sally crying? Sally was crying because Sally had experienced rejection. She had become an outcast. And, again, like I said earlier, this has become quite the norm in our society – the whole outcast concept and how we should just be lucky we're not one of them OR how we should just stay quiet if we are.

Rejection means to be cast aside, outcast. Rejection means to be thrown away as if you have no value. To be rejected is to be told, "I don't want you, and you don't have any value." Rejection or to be outcast or cast aside means you are not wanted – you are not what is needed – you don't matter. Rejection seems to solidify for most people the fact that there is just something "not right" about that person – about that outcast – and that he or she is not worthy or deserving of help or inclusion.

Rejection is, in fact, one of the key masterpieces of satanic oppression. Rejection is truly also the most untreated illness within the body of Christ. Whenever a person experiences rejection of any form and on any stage, he or she tends to build up walls. Rejection is really just a symptom in this illness, for it is really a combination of abuse, guilt, identity issues, and perceived public as well as self-image. Rejection, or being an outcast, hinders the believer from ever experiencing full love, peace, joy, and grace. After all, if people aren't included with others on a daily basis or if stories and gossip run rampant or even if perception of an individual becomes a misguided reality, of course these people will begin to reject societal norms, including God's love and the warm embrace of the church. Rejection, therefore, is a collection of chains that can potentially wrap itself around us due to something that has, perhaps, happened to us in the past (that shame that we alluded to in previous chapters). In this way, we often ostracize ourselves, assume that we are unworthy or unloved or feel that others do not want to spend time with us.

Now, you'll notice, I have gradually pulled us from the schoolyard, where we once stood, either the insecure recipient of some terrible nursery rhyme or the misguided follower, too afraid to stand up for the perceived "outcast", to our current adult lives, where, for many of us, those feelings of isolation and shame still engulf us and make us feel rejected. And, this rejection comes in all forms, doesn't it? Maybe you've experienced the untimely death of a loved one, and those around you don't know what to do or to say in the wake of this terrible tragedy. For you, the victim in all this, maybe this was the person who you thought would grow old with you. And, now, maybe, as you make your transition from a single person against the world, without your beloved partner, you feel the awkward distance from others, and maybe they feel it too.

Maybe you nurtured and loved a child his or her whole life only to bury your sweet angel before his or her time. Standing in the aftermath of the unthinkable – burying your child, crying bitter tears, wanting help from others to bring closure to something you thought you would never see – burying someone that you brought into the world – maybe you feel frozen, you don't know where to go, who to reach out to. As thoughts race through your mind – that you always thought he or she would bury you in old age – that you have a bedroom for him or her that you've had in your house for years, full of clothes and artwork and photos from that child's life that will now sit empty – that those around you are so horrified by what has happened that no one will ever address the issue with you – you may begin to already feel rejected and alone.

I spoke to a young woman one time who had just had her second child, and her story really touched me. Her baby had been born with a heart condition, and her mother was battling cancer at the same time. She, herself, had some complications during pregnancy, and… while she was recovering in the hospital, her mother weak from chemotherapy but trying to help her, and her baby whisked away by ambulance to a critical care unit at the children's hospital, she was visited by her mother in-law and her sister in-law, who proceeded to verbally abuse her. They told her that this second baby would financially hurt her family – that her mother's illness was a burden on their son and brother – and that she, now ailing and trying to recover, would be useless – unable to cook or clean for her family. They even went as far to suggest that they take the preschooler already at home, since she was so incapacitated and, obviously, overwhelmed. Understandably, she was hurt – shocked, confused, and frightened by it all. Later, she discovered that the mother in law had become jealous of her mother, who was spending so much time with the family – the children, etc. – and that her own 30-year marriage was breaking up. She also learned that her sister-in-law had been suffering with infertility issues for years but had hidden it from everyone. Once she heard this, she was able to be the one to reach out and mend the rift that was already making them all feel rejected and outcast from the family. By understanding and being the bigger person, she could forgive and try to open up again – for her family and for her overall relationship with God.

Some of you, as children, might have been left alone so often by caregivers that somewhere in your mind and your spirit, you now seem to be only content when you are by yourselves and that keeps you from pursuing friendships and other relationships. For some of us, somebody, maybe a parent, left you with a terrible scar, telling you over and over again that you are never going to be anything, or calling you dumb or stupid. And, these are things that we can't control. And, truthfully, they don't make us rejects at all, but it is hard to make that leap – from downtrodden, hurt, confused child – to clear-thinking, confident adult. Again, I met another young woman who had always known that her brothers were her mother's favorites and, as a result, as a grown person, felt that she was not attractive, could not get a good job, and was so unlovable that no one would ever want her. Of course, this was not true and, after some time away from this neglectful situation, she was able to see her strengths – among them rising above such abuse and rejection – and she was finally able to focus on her inner and outer beauty and all that she could offer the world.

For some of us, as young children, we were touched by someone inappropriately, so now as adults, we are afraid to allow anybody to really touch us because we can still feel that vile or nasty touch – we can't trust anyone – and, again, we don't feel worthy of love or warmth and security. And, yet again, such an atrocity in our life is not one that we chose, invited, or were in any way responsible for, but... still, the hurt, confusion, and, yes, the rejection from society is apparent. How do we change that? How do we rise above something so damaging yet so independent of who we really are? It is difficult.

Anyone will tell you that any kind of rejection – the denial of a close friendship – the rejection of a parent or a child – or an event for which we may, mistakenly, feel responsible, like a divorce or an incestuous, inappropriate relationship – will make anyone feel down, sad, dejected, and, in some cases, unable to move on. You can live among people yet feel like you're worlds apart from anyone else, and this is terrible – a gripping, polarizing fear – a daunting task to try to overcome it all.

We touched on divorce a bit in the last unit. And, now, as we find ourselves exploring events that we may feel responsible for keeping us from joining society and feeling like less of an outcast, it rears its problematic, ugly head again. As you know, divorce is rampant in this country. Whether we know someone who has experienced it or experienced it ourselves, it touches us all in some way. And, divorce, truly does speak volumes to you in terms of making you feel that you are not wanted, so don't discount it as something that you have done or contributed to;

make sure you embrace the facts that you can move on, and you can put it behind you. And, remember, divorce takes all forms; that young woman who had her in-laws attack her verbally probably felt divorced from them for a time. That child who just knew her family preferred her brothers over her experienced a divorce of sorts. Anytime you have given your all to a person or a situation, revealed all of your strengths and weaknesses and given everything you had, it will hurt when that rejection – that "I don't care if I hurt you" or "I don't want you anymore" happens. And when the divorce is the break-up of a marriage, and you did choose that person and presume to build a life with him or her, and they choose someone else, that pain is as real as it gets. Suddenly, this person who you so trusted now wants someone else. Now after so many years of a relationship or marriage, somebody else is sitting in the car you bought, living in the house you decorated, sleeping in the bed you made up, and you have concluded that you will never trust nor love again because you have been rejected, you are an outcast. You made a choice and you chose wrong, and now you can't even trust yourself. Outcast. Rejected.

And, why do we do this to ourselves? Yes, it is hard to rise above the scorn of others, and it is difficult to move past the terrible things that life can send our way. But to actually ostracize ourselves is a sad thing. Why try to look like everyone else? Why try to act like everyone else? Why should we care what others think?

> *.... it also helps to begin to heal yourself – focusing on your strengths, what you have overcome instead of your weaknesses and what you have endured.*

Experiencing any of these traumas either as a child or an adult, victims subconsciously position themselves into several different areas. They may continue to allow themselves to be abused over and over again, and they may even become abusers – either unconsciously or actively. Others, who have experienced rejection or pain, may begin to inflict pain on themselves, in effect punishing themselves for being a "bad" child – a child who wasn't "liked" by his parents or others. I see this often when I have young people who come to me and tell me that they cut themselves or hurt themselves in other ways – through eating disorders or substance abuse. And, for all this, it takes a long time to turn around these conflicted feelings. It helps to reach out to others – churches, doctors, friends – but it also helps to begin to heal yourself – on your strengths, what you have overcome instead of your weaknesses and what you have endured.

All rejection is difficult, and I do see all kinds. From how we look to people's sexual preference, the potential for rejection – even from family and loved ones – is great. And, once that rejection creeps outside the home – to your place of work, your school, even your church, – the damage to an individual's psyche can be almost irreparable. After all, when you're judged, for example, by the color of your skin as opposed to the strength of your character again and again, it will begin to wear on you, and.... understandably so. The challenge becomes, then, to rise above it all and move forward. It is sad to see the opposite – when people have become so down that they can't get up or, worse, that they have begun to act out and reject others in return. After reaching out for solace to friends and family or going to the church for shelter from this rejection only to be turned away or ignored – even if this rejection is just perceived – can do terrible things to a person. The example the victims then set for others is not good, and the cycle continues.

Basically, rejection has two sides. It has the side of the one who caused the rejection and the other side is the one who experienced the rejection. In this book, we want to address both and offer grace to both victims –those who caused the pain and rejection and those who were the recipients. And if God can heal the person who experienced rejection, surely He can heal the person who caused it.

 You and I are not the first to experience rejection or be outcast. Our Biblical text, Genesis 21, introduces us to a parent as well as a child who had similar experiences. Would you journey with me as we examine their plight and see what we can learn from their experience so we may gain insight on how we too can become, "Unshackled from the Spirit of Rejection" AND dance with the spirit of acceptance? Let me say that while all rejection of any kind is very painful, there is nothing like the rejection of a parent – A father who wants nothing to do with a child or a mother who turns her back on her own child. Child rejection, as I have personally witnessed, has had an impact on me in my adulthood.

Let me also say at the very beginning that it amazes me that the story of a person experiencing rejection or being outcast is found in the book of Genesis, which is the book of beginnings. It is suggesting to you and to me that we are not the first, nor will we be the last to experience any form of rejection. Remember, the Bible said "There is nothing new under the sun" (Eccl. 1:9).

In Genesis, Chapter 16, we are introduced to a man and wife who most of us should be familiar with – Abraham. Abraham was married to Sarah, and the Lord had made a promise to Abraham and Sarah that they would have a child in their old age and the child will be the promised one – the one that God would bless Abraham and Sarah for generations to come. Of course Sarah grew inpatient with God when she did not become pregnant. After all, one year, five years, and ten years had gone, and Abraham and Sarah were not getting any younger. In fact, they were getting older in years; Sarah, as well as Abraham, was pushing seventy. In her haste, Sarah decided to take matters into her own hands by suggesting to Abraham that, because God was taking so long to fulfill his promise, maybe they should help God out. Not that they didn't trust Him or not that they were second-guessing anything, they just wanted to fulfill the mission that God had intended for them. She suggested, or rather commanded, that Abraham go in and lay with Sarah's maid, Hagar, who was an Egyptian (Genesis 16:1).

The account of this story, as controversial as it may seem to us now is rich with meaning and personal applications. Abraham honors this request, goes in to Hagar, and they produce a child by the name of Ishmael. Ishmael represents in scripture the one that God allowed. He is known as the permitted one. Ishmael represents the permitted will of God in the life of Abraham and Sarah. Twenty-five years later, Abraham and Sarah do have a child together – Isaac. Isaac, by contrast, represents the perfect will of God. After all, God permitted the birth of Ishmael to give Sarah and Abraham what they felt they needed, and now He has, as promised, produced a child for them as was His plan – thereby making Isaac the result of His "perfect" will. It is important to note here that the birth of one son occurred because man was impatient and the birth of the other son occurred because God was faithful and fulfilled His promise. This clearly represents a God who may not always come when you want Him to, but He will come when the time is right.

It is also important to note here that this phenomenon suggests that some things that happen to us in our lives are not the perfect will of God, but God did permit them because they must be part of our individual journey for some reason. Of course, God allows things to happen because, while He is all-powerful, He cannot interrupt man's free will. You and I have free will, which means God will not force us to do anything that we don't want to do. We make our own choices, and we set our own paths – good or bad. Of course, again, sometimes we are the victims of free will gone wrong and other times, we are the perpetrators – sometimes acting in accordance with God's plan – other times opposing it or doing wrong.

Everything we do has repercussions. Just as we live with injustice that is no fault of our own, we also live with our own bad or misguided decisions. By contrast, we also live with our good decisions. The good and the bad. We have to accept it all.

God is not out to punish us, but there are natural as well as spiritual consequences to every action. If you sell drugs and get caught and have to serve jail time, you must realize that this is not God punishing you; it is the natural consequences of your own actions. The Bible says, "Whatsoever a man sows that shall he also reap" (Gal. 6:7). If you have sex and do not use protection and either get pregnant or contract an infection; that is not God judging you because you had sex, it is the natural consequences of the decisions you made. Whatever you sow, you will reap; what goes around comes around. What goes up must come down. These are all just natural, logical principles of existence and responsibility. Once we understand that, it becomes easier to do what we need to do to correct our mistakes and live with our choices. That doesn't mean we have to accept a terrible fate, but it does mean we are partially responsible for the way we go in life – bad luck, abuse, rejection and all.

> *God is not out to punish us, but there are natural*
> *as well as spiritual consequences to every action.*

The Bible says in Matthew 5:45 that "the rain falls on the just as well as the unjust". In other words, just because you are in church and love the Lord does not mean you are exempt from the consequences of your actions. The only difference is that a child of God has a grace factor. And Paul said, what shall we say then? Shall we continue in sin that grace may abound? (Romans 6:1) Grace is God giving you what you don't deserve and mercy is God holding back what you do deserve. It helps to have all this in perspective when we all do our self-examinations.

While we see the permitted and perfect will of God in our text, often we still can't accept that dichotomy. In fact, for some of us, we stagnate, trying to make sense of the same in our own lives and, yet, we continue to live in the permitted will and not the perfect will of our own lives. For example, we marry a person – good or bad, and we get pregnant, making life a little bit harder. Maybe we realize our partner is not who he or she said he was – maybe we feel that we've made a mistake – and, now, doing what we think is right, caring for and loving a child, we wonder why God is allowing us to suffer in a loveless marriage or why He is making the simplest tasks – cooking, working, driving to daycare – so trying. And, of course, none of this is God; this is all the consequence of a wrong choice or a bad decision. Abraham and Sarah made a decision, and they had to live with the decision they made, the choices they made. We've all experienced this before – living with a bad decision or a wrong choice. Many times, we wish we could roll back the hands of time, but we can't. In truth, we have to find a better, more viable option. So – do we just pray the way we've been taught to? Do we change our path? Do we accept our decisions as well as the plan God has set forth for us? Yes. We all know the serenity prayer; sometimes it is time to live it. "God, grant me the serenity to accept the things I cannot change; courage to change the things I can; and wisdom to know the difference." (Reinhold Niebuhr, Theologian, sermon date: 1943)

The Bible says that, after twenty-five years of waiting for God to fulfill the promise, Sarah finally had a child by the name of Isaac. What God permitted earlier – the birth of Ishmael – did not stop God's perfect will. Life was a little bit harder; what had been permitted due to an ill-advised decision slowed down progress a bit for Sarah and Abraham, but did not stop the promise. Let me say also that, in the theological world, both boys represent a typology. Ishmael is the son of the flesh, and Isaac is the promise of the Spirit. Please note here that both children do have value. A bad decision doesn't produce a bad child. That child born of a bad marriage that we talked about earlier was a blessing to his or her mother too; these simple details we need to remember to spur us onto better things. Now, the

Bible says, "Both boys grew side by side". On one occasion, Sarah decided to have a birthday party for Isaac, and as they were celebrating his birthday, Sarah saw Ishmael, the permitted one, laughing at the perfect one and she was upset. So she tells Abraham in Genesis 21:10, "Wherefore," she said unto Abraham, "cast out this bondwoman and her son for the bondwoman and her son will not be heir with my son." In other words, Abraham had to, basically, get rid of them, cast them aside, throw them out or away as if they have no value. I don't want them and they have no value to us. We don't need her or her child; we have our own now.

Now when I first read this text I thought Sarah was being a little hard and overly protective of Isaac. After all, it seemed like these boys were just being boys and taunting one another. But once I researched it further, I realized that there is more to it – that something deeper lies beneath it all. Ishmael was considerably older than Isaac, and when children are together, the elder should be careful and more tender of the younger. In this case, it almost appears that Ishmael was being abusive to a child who was no way his peer. In this way, Ishmael is an abuser – though, we can assume that he probably never enjoyed the same privileges as the son born of God's perfect will. Here we see the victim / abuser dichotomy in action.

Now, in this case, the Bible says that Abraham was grieved and yet he honored Sarah's request. The next day, Abraham woke up early and took bread and a bottle of water to Hagar and his first son, Ishmael. In a way, he is bringing them what, today, we would refer to as child support, yet leaves the responsibility of caring for a child alone to Hagar. And the Bible said she departed and wandered in the wilderness or wild-ness of Beersheba. And that's where rejection leads you; it will leave you in a wandering state, in a wilderness. A place where you are asking yourself over and over again why? What did I do wrong? Hagar did not do anything wrong and neither did Ishmael. And that's the first impression I want to make to those of you who have experienced rejection. Don't assume that the rejection you experience was because of something you've done. Sometimes it's about you, but, most of the time, it is not. Rejection makes you wonder: Was I not good enough? Rejection gets to the core of your self image for it tells you that you are not valued; you are worthless, only worth a piece of bread and a bottle of water. Some of us, again because of either childhood rejection or rejection as adults, are wandering in the wilderness. We are wandering from one relationship to another – from one job to another – from one drug to another – from one church to another – and beyond; we have become only wanderers. Our souls have no anchor. For some of us, we end up like Hagar, wandering all of our lives and asking, "Why me?" or "What did I do wrong?" "Why did my mother or father give me up for adoption?" "Why did my marriage end in a divorce?" And some of us, we are not wandering in the wilderness, but we are dying in the wilderness; we are simply girls and boys gone wild. And, we need to realize that maybe we were given up for adoption but we found a loving family or forged our own path, and maybe our marriage did end in divorce but maybe we are now better for it, smarter, more savvy, and ready to truly love someone again.

Now, as alluded to in the Bible, wilderness also implies "wild-ness". This is why some of you, at 14, you have already had as many sexual partners as an adult. At 18, you are on your second or third child. At 25, you have already contracted an infection, and at 30, you have already had two abortions. It's because you are now wandering in the wilderness. You are all out of bread and water; you have lost the essence of who you are.

There are several areas of modern day "wilderness" that rejection can potentially make you hostage to. The first is insecurity. In this circle of sorts, you will never find satisfaction. You may begin to speak negative things that become your realities and the perceived realities of others. You'll begin to believe that everyone is "better" than you are. You will compare yourself to everyone else. You may find yourself in a relationship in which the other person has to know your every move and you excuse it because you understand that type of insecurity, and the cycle continues.

The second area is the circle or "wilderness" of intimidation. In this circle, you are uncomfortable with success and the compliments of others. You really don't mean to be this way – in fact, most of us would consciously say we want to be complimented, but, once trapped in this area, it seems that getting ahead or getting the attention makes you uncomfortable and, so, subconsciously, you begin to undermine yourself. Just beyond these endless circles of insecurity and intimidation is the circle of isolation. In this circle, you are more comfortable when you are alone because you have built up layer upon layer of falsity. You have hidden yourself under layers of insulation. You've built walls behind walls and nobody can get in!

Somebody may want to love you, get to know you, include you – but the walls have to come down.

Now, back to the story of Abraham and Sarah: the text said, "When the water was spent and the bread was gone that Hagar cast the child under one of the shrubs" (Genesis 21:15). Have we all become desensitized to rejection as in the taunting nursery rhyme I spoke of previously? Is this type of rejection so embedded in society that we can't see it? We miss it even in our Bible verse? In Verse 10, Sarah told Abraham and cast Hagar out (Genesis 21:10). As Hagar is wandering in the wilderness, she, in return, casts out her own flesh and blood. She cast him under a tree. To bring the perspective to modern day, she cast him into a foster home. She cast him into a potentially unhealthy environment because she is repeating what she had seen or experienced. Most people who reject or devalue another human being do so because they have been rejected or devalued themselves. Now, again Ishmael, the child, did nothing wrong. He is the only innocent person in this party – but he is suffering because of a series of decisions made by adults, presumably people who know better.

I usually get to minister to adults and, often, in my speeches and sermons, do take the opportunity to say to the children: My young people, who have been blaming themselves for their parents' divorce or their parents' issues, in general – please do not think that either has anything to do with you. Your parents may have rejected one another, but they do not wish to reject you. And, if you do feel pain as a result of something an adult did, do not blame yourself. That rejection is not your fault. You are caught in the crossfire; you are an innocent bystander. And this does happen.

Hagar is the person who had been cast out, and suddenly she becomes the one who casts out her own family. And, it seems this is true, in the case of Hagar and her son, Ishmael: "She did not think she had what it took to keep him alive and she did not want to see him die." For personal application: Those of you who have been adopted and think you were put up for adoption because your mother did not love you, consider the case of Hagar and her beloved son. She did what she felt she had to do – what she had learned. Please – those of you who are adopted –remember that you were given up for adoption and adopted because your biological mother did love you and she did not believe she had what it took to keep you alive and she did not want you to die. And we know, in the Bible, that Hagar did not want to cast Ishmael aside because the Bible said she lifted up her voice and wept. The text says, "And the Lord heard the voice of the lad" (Genesis 21:17). This means that while she is crying, the lad is also lifting up his voice. And, again, to the young people: do you know what that means? You can intercede on behalf of your parents. You can intercede on your own behalf. Have faith that God is listening, and in this case, God not only hears the voice of the lad, but God dispatches an angel to minister to his mother. The angel asks her what is wrong and proceeds to help. All is never lost, is it?

Now, to Hagar, the angel says, "Fear not, for God has heard the voice of the lad." He said, "Arise, lift up the lad and hold him for I will make him a great nation" (Genesis 21:18). And God opens her eyes and she sees a well of water and she goes to the well and she fills the bottle with water and gives the lad drink. And he dwells in the wilderness. Notice, he does not die but dwells – becomes productive – an anchor– somebody. Hagar and Ishmael become "unshackled from rejection." They did not allow what happened in their past to hinder their progress nor kill their future. You, too, can be unshackled from past and present rejection.

And, I'm sure you're asking: How, then, do I become "unshackled from rejection?" How do I shake loose the wounds and scars and pain of rejection? First and foremost, to become "unshackled from rejection", you are going to have to have enough faith to rise above it. In verse 18, "arise" means to get up". Rejection can paralyze you in such a way that you can go into a deep depression; you can wallow in self -pity. You can feel like your world is out of control. You can lose your strength, your focus, and your joy of living. And because of that, the last thing on your mind is getting up. You would rather stay where you are. You are stuck in the event or situation or wilderness, but you are going to have to have faith to rise. You have to move from crying over things that you cannot do anything about to changing and improving things in your control. You are going to have to move, to rise. Notice that faith is active. You can, by faith, rise above that which is hanging over your head.

Second, you are going to have to learn how to forgive. Notice Hagar never went back. She learned to forgive. And to forgive is the hardest step.

To forgive means to let it go. It carries the meaning of unmerited favor, meaning that, often, these people do not deserve forgiveness, but you do extend it to them – to move on and to live better. Forgiveness is not about the other person; it's about you extending to that person unmerited favor. Notice I say you have to learn to forgive, which means it will not come to you over night – you have to learn and think and get to that place that makes you comfortable with it. Forgiveness is the act of setting somebody free from an obligation, and, in turn setting yourself free from a wrongful situation, an injustice. For example, a debt is forgiven when you free your debtor of the obligation of paying back what he owes. Those people who have hurt you in the past and are hurting you now will continue to do so unless you forgive them. You see, Abraham and Sarah had gone on with their lives. Hagar could not allow them to hinder her by carrying unforgiveness. To forgive means we have to deal with all the necessary steps that happen to us when we have been hurt or experienced rejection.

Finally, if we are going to become "unshackled from rejection", we must learn to make the best out of a bad situation. While what happened to Hagar and Ishmael was not the perfect will of God, they learned to make the very best out of the situation. What happened was not good but God took all of it and worked it all together for their good (Romans 8:28). This is the living with the good and the bad that I want you all to realize.

Look at the good things that came out of this bad situation. Hagar got a vision for her life. The Bible said her eyes were opened. (Genesis 21:18) Sometimes it is in going through so much that seems so difficult that your eyes are opened. In the 1970s, President Gerald Ford said, after pardoning President Richard Nixon on Watergate, that Nixon had said to him, "Everyone calls you when you win, but only your friends call you when you fail." And sometimes, it's in the midst of a messed up situation, that your eyes are opened. You can see clearly your destiny and your purpose.

Notice, the text said, "The boy grew." (Genesis 21:20) You are going to have to learn and grow from the situation or circumstance. In spite of the pain and rejection, the boy, Ishmael, grew. And we call this 'growing pains'. In fact, it is said that you are most dangerous to the devil when you're in the middle of a mess, a difficult situation, because, in that case, you are still growing and becoming more powerful. Remember that. And remember, too, that spiritual growth is not in the absence of trials and pain, but, rather, spiritual growth is in the midst of a mess — those trials and pain. If you want to know what you are made of, evaluate yourself when you are in the valley — experiencing the trials and tribulations of life, in the lion's den — not when you are on the mountaintop, experiencing life's rewards. Anybody can praise God and sing and preach when all is going well. Anybody can talk about how they love their leaders when all is going well, but it's another thing when a mess is going on.

Finally, we can take from the text the following: "The lad grew because God was with him. And he became an anchor." (Verse 20) He became productive and not destructive. He found his purpose, his destiny. It said, "The Lord was with him and he dwelled." (Genesis 21:20) Not died, but dwelled–became productive in the wilderness and his mama took him a wife from Egypt. In other words, he became "unshackled from rejection" for production. You cannot be productive until you are willing to let the spirit of rejection loose in your life. You cannot be productive until you let go of trying to be destructive. In the midst of all of that the text said, "And his mother took him a wife from Egypt" (Genesis 21:21). He was free to love and be loved again. And this is certainly something that we are all worthy of and capable of achieving. He was free to dance even with his brokenness.

To Shed Rejection and to Dance Like a Star: An Epilogue to Unit Two

Nothing I have brought up in the preceding unit is easy. It is hard to acknowledge when we've been hurt, and it is hard to step up and take the opportunity to become better. When we feel rejected and alone, that is when we feel the weakest. And, in the close of Unit 2, as I remind you all to relish those times of trial — when you can truly show what you're made of and emerge in triumph, unscathed and smiling, I do realize the gravity of what I'm asking you to do.

In the previous epilogue, I asked you to record some initiatives for future examination — maybe when you finish this book — maybe in a few months, when you feel like tackling your "to do" list. In this epilogue, however, I'm going to ask you to simply do this one quick exercise — to look in the mirror — confess what you think is the worst thing you've ever done or experienced to your own reflection –then… without missing a beat, I want you to tell yourself what you do well and verbalize one thing that you have to look forward to in the coming days, weeks or months. Now, take out that phone, that camera, or that pad of paper, and take a picture of yourself in this moment or jot down your feelings in this moment. Keep this photo, this list of thoughts – whatever it is – and put it somewhere safe. When you're having a bad day or when someone makes you feel terrible, I want you to take it out – and look at it – that smiling photo, replete with confidence – that person who just confessed something troubling yet reaffirmed life and determination by mentioning something positive. This is your starting point – the start to a fantastic life choreographed using the best and the worst of your experiences.

Paste that photo or that list of "good thoughts" below:

A LETTER
FROM DR. JAZZ

Choreographing a Life by Dancing with Broken Bones: A Letter from Dr. Jazz

Dear Gentle Readers,

Well, we're midway there. We're in the throes of battling ourselves and those around us for the opportunity to dance the dance of praise – the dance that will celebrate the richness of our lives and what makes us uniquely the people we are. And, this is hard, isn't it? Discovering what we want out of life and, then, mustering the courage to achieve it all in the way that we know we can.

I have challenged you with a variety of tasks and life-changing perspectives. While you may feel overwhelmed by it all, look more closely at what I'm asking you to do. I simply want you to break any destructive patterns of abuse towards yourself and others, and I want you to begin to totally accept the person that you are – no matter what that entails – bad credit, good cooking, devoted mothering, recovering from alcoholism, going back to school, etc. – everything from the color of your eyes to your favorite movie – from your past with bad behavior to your future as a happy, fulfilled person. It's really not that hard; it just takes some forward thinking.

I have challenged you with a variety of tasks and life-changing perspectives.

I have heard countless stories from people who will tell me that anytime they met a person who was helpful or inspiring to them, it was always someone who had been through a lot – the guy in the street who shares with you his story of addiction and recovery and his new lease on life that involves travel and new positive relationships – that pastor who listened to your deepest darkest secrets in a private, confessional setting and, instead of judging, asked you to be a teacher, an example to kids in the church for rising above difficulties – that chef at the new restaurant down the street who shares with you, as you sit alone in the dining room wishing you had a dinner companion, that, at one time, she had to support six kids with no degree and no money and no partner in life – and yet now stands proud as a successful business owner with a full, rich life. Maybe it was just the older woman who asked to share a table with you at the coffee shop and, instead of finding her lonely or helpless, you find her company and her enthusiasm for life refreshing and enlightening. Or that young man, the one that everyone said was "no good", who helps you carry your groceries into the house and tells you that he works for the Food Bank every holiday season. This young man – the one who once was in jail and, once out, is being productive in reaching out and giving back to the community in which he once used to sell drugs with no regard for anyone but himself. What tremendous success stories these people are!

...inspiration comes in all forms...

I have come to understand that inspiration comes in all forms, from people of different colors and cultures. In that way, your challenge is easy and, in a way, rather fun. You get to seek out interesting people – explore that side of yourself that is exciting and inspired – and, above all, choreograph yourself a plan – a dance – a life – worthy of YOU. So continue reading, continue learning, begin exploring, and eventually go forth to make God, your friends and family, and yourselves happy! Go ahead and start dancing.

With you on the dance floor –
Dr. Jazz

UNIT III

Unshackled from Un-forgiveness:
Learning to Extend Forgiveness,
Comfort, and Restoration
to Yourself and Others

2 Corinthians 2:5

When we talk about forgiveness, we tend to focus on the person who has experienced the wrong and his or her willingness to forgive another person. The emphasis is placed on the victim, the person who was the recipient of the pain, the hurt or the hate. However, I believe in the circle of relationships, that relationships are built on mutual intimacy and trust, and then, often, that relationship will be tested. Given that, I believe that, in every unfortunate situation involving the inability to forgive or even the act of hurting, there are at least two victims — many times, even more. The road to testing sometimes begins when someone in the relationship is offended, whether that offense is intentional or unintentional. If the person who has been offended does not address it properly, then he or she may move from hurt, which is sometimes in the form of detachment, onto hate, which is always damaging, bitter, and then harmful, especially when hate turns to vengeance. When any of us has been offended, we often don't deal with it properly, and, despite knowing better, we move from hurt, to hate, and to harm, even if the offense was intentional or unintentional. Also, because we, when wounded, often move so quickly to hurt and detachment — pain and hatred - we never really travel the road of grieving, which is an important step in the process to nurture our relationships. We obsess over the hurt that was caused to us, and we never move freely into grieving and embracing that hurt — trying to do something productive with it; therefore, we also never reach the confrontation stage, also an important step or role in the development of our personal relationships.

Many of us, as Christians, and non Christians do not like confrontation - have even been told to stay away from confrontation — so we do tend to associate it with repressed rage or angry altercations; therefore, instead of healing and restoration in these temporarily damaged relationships, there is disunity, distrust and the relationship never gets restored or moves back to a healthy stage. All of us have the tendency to sweep things under a rug or pretend that nothing ever happened. Often, we lash out. All of this comes from hurt that has been converted to repressed rage — all because we don't address the issues, the relationship or the person when we should. The Bible tells us in Ephesians 4:26 , "Be ye angry, but sin not, and do not let the sin go down on your wrath." Anger is not bad - it is an indication that you have been hurt. We learn that you control anger but rage controls you.

Now, in this life, you and I know we will never be able to avoid offending people and people offending us. All of us, from the pulpit to the pew, have offended and have been offended by someone even if the offense was unintentional. Jesus said it so clearly in Luke 17:1. He said, "It is impossible but that offenses will come." If you are in any kind of relationship, a relationship between a husband and a wife, a parent and a child, a boss and an employee, and even a relationship between a pastor and a congregation – there will be instances when offenses will take place, feelings will be hurt, people will feel "un-forgiven", so to speak, or be unwilling to forgive. Whether any of this is intentional or unintentional, it can all occur even in the closest of friendships.

There have been times in which I am sure I may have inadvertently offended someone, and there have been times when I have been wholeheartedly offended – by family, friends, even my congregation. Again, this is the type of road where relationships are tested. Relationships that have not been tested in this way may have issues; the very fact that they have not walked the road of pain and either intentional or unintentional harm may be an indication that someone in the relationship is not being honest about what he or she feels or thinks. In that way, the intimacy that should exist may not exist. People in relationships do not handle everything the same way or even see things the same way – no matter how close they feel to the other party in the relationship. And… this is normal. This facilitates true intimacy and sets up the situation for true confidence and sharing. Throughout all of our lives, we will see offense in marriages, in relationships, in friendships, and, yes, we will see it in the church, which is also a type of intimate family for us. Remember, we are not simply in relationships with God, but we are in relationships with each other. Of course, with such a broad field to handle, our relationships will be tested in some way in our lifetime.

In a church and in life, we are, basically, brothers and sisters - we are family. And we know that no one can hurt us as much as family, those who are closest to you. In our church family, we are closely connected because we have the same father. And, as is the case with our families at home, there are disagreements, conflicts, and offenses. Why would you think that it would not happen in the church? Of course, when we do have conflicts with family and friends, we turn to the church, which makes it that much harder when our conflict – our issue – is with that supposed sanctuary of forgiveness and comfort. Then – the issue becomes more than just the offense or what we perceive as the offense – we've been excluded, someone said something about us, we've seen others enjoy more success – but, as children of God, children of the Most High, children of the Light – it becomes how we handle our response. Do we move forward? Do we forgive? Do we change? Do we confront the offender? And, above all, how do we do this all with so much pain – so hurt and confused?

In a church and in life, we are, basically, brothers and sisters - we are family.

Many times, when we have been hurt, we tap into that world mentality that is so prevalent and that tells us to hurt those who have hurt us. Sometimes, it is easy to feel that – if the world can't see my pain then I will make it feel my pain. And, this, as we've been discussing, is not productive. It is not what God wants for us. In fact, the issue for the child of God is not being hurt – because we all will be, living in such a sinful and fallen world – but it is, as we said before, how we deal with this hurt. Many of us, instead of allowing the offense to become a stepping-stone, have allowed the offense to become a stumbling block. Instead of us healing, we go on living with a hurt. Listen brothers and sisters, God cannot heal what we concealed. Rather than taking the step of Godly conformation so the relationship may be restored, we take the road of denial, which leads to detachment, bitterness, and vengeance. Furthermore, we go through life with un-forgiveness. Whenever we house un-forgiveness in our heart, we hinder the full move of God to operate in our lives.

Now that we've examined, in part, the victim's feelings of pain and, often, retribution, let's take a look at the other side – the offender's point of view – the one who caused the hurt. As I said earlier, being hurt, being forgiven, offering forgiveness, and casting aside hatred and vengeance are all two-sided concepts. These relationships harmed by offenses, either intentional or unintentional, are two-sided, multi-faceted, both human and divine relationships that require honesty and open-ness.

Of course, we all know that one of the greatest gifts we can give someone is the gift of forgiveness. It is, in fact, the responsibility of the faith community to extend forgiveness to those in our household of worship. In looking at the offender's side in addition to the victim's, however, we climb a slippery slope. After all, how easy is it for any of us right now to imagine forgiving some of these people – people who cause the pain, pull the trigger, if you will – hold the gun that caused all the pain? It isn't easy. It is truly a challenge. If, however, we look at the facts, we see that the person who causes the pain often holds all the power over the person receiving the pain. Again, this is not a healthy dynamic. To effectively address the issue, we can't forget and brush it under the rug, so to speak. And if we do not address, rebuke, and confront the person who caused the pain or the offense then we are suggesting that the victim is the only one with the pain. And if the truth is told, both have experienced some form of pain. Remember, people in pain hurt others, so try to remember that when someone hurts another, it is likely they have been hurt themselves in some way. This is one of the reasons that we cannot forget the offender.

Of course, we all know that one of the greatest gifts we can give someone is the gift of forgiveness.

The Christian Bible has a therapy for the one who caused the pain and it also has a therapy for the victims of such pain. The Bible, in fact, first deals with the one who caused the pain. In 2 Corinthians, we find information that suggests that we do need to minister to the person who caused the pain. We need to note that Paul, the apostle who laid it out this way, had caused others pain and knew, firsthand, that he had been hurt in the past, and that he could no longer go on infecting an entire community with his pain. His idea, therefore, was to deal with the offender, purge the pain and hurtful behavior from the community, then administer to the victims who have not caused pain and move forward. In this way, he was dealing with trying to rid the community of what we now call "bullying". As we all know, when someone turns out to be a bully, it is usually because they have been bullied themselves.

Paul and his Pain

Paul, in 2 Corinthians, gives us an emotional therapy to administer to those who frequently cause the pain. In Corinthians, Paul is directing his comments to a church rich in gifts of the spirit. This church had the gift of prophecy, the gift of teaching, the gift of exhortation, the gift of speaking in tongues, the gifts of healing – in fact, it seemed that they had all the gifts. As a very gifted and talented church, they were truly blessed. However, they lacked the fruits of the spirit, and, as we know, the "fruits" referenced in the Bible are very different than the "gifts". In fact, in this church they were one of the most gifted and talented churches, but they lacked the fruits of the spirit. They emphasized the gifts of the spirit so much that they never allowed the Lord to develop the fruits of the spirit within their church. As we all know, "the fruits of the spirit, which are love, joy, peace, gentleness, faith, meekness, temperance, against such there is no law" (Galatians 5: 22 – 23) and all those enviable qualities of character that sometimes take quite a bit of work and soul-searching.

So, this church at Corinth had all the gifts, but, in truth, they fought like cats and dogs. They fought over the smallest things – like we do now in the modern world when we have forgotten to grow and flow in the fruit of the spirit – over the color of the carpet, who talks to who, who is the better cook, who does more for the church, etc. They might have even fought over who was supposed to sit in a certain seat in worship. And… we all know this type of behavior, don't we? We see this in our daily lives now and then. In fact, in this most gifted church, every imaginable sin was present. And the Corinth church became known as a carnal, immature church.

To provide a little background on this church: In AD 40. Paul went to preach at Corinth, eventually forming and developing this Church of Corinth. The Bible tells us that the Church at Corinth was made up of predominantly poor or lower class people. However, after Paul's preaches, those from the upper class become intrigued and eventually convert and join the Corinth church. So the church remained mainly poor but had a few elite, wealthy, and educated people. There were a few in the Corinth church that, in modern terms, had a Bachelor's degree, a Master's, or a Ph.D., and Paul had a Doctor of Ministry. For Paul, this was the first time in his ministry that people from the upper class had ever joined the church. Paul's preaching attracted poor people, but now the middle class and the upper class were joining this congregation, which, of course, began to change the dynamic a bit, bringing about new sets of problems between the "haves" and the "have nots" or the upper and the lower classes.

In 2 Corinthians 1:12-16, we are introduced to four of the wealthiest people in the Corinth church. Out of the four of them is a woman, Cleo. Now, as the church was established in Corinth, the congregation needed a place to worship, and sure enough, one of the wealthy people, Gaius, hosted and housed the Corinth church. The Biblical text tells us that after Paul preached and established the Corinth church, he traveled to Macedonia, leaving room for a new pastor/teacher whose name was Apollos. The lower class within that congregation loved Paul because they could relate to him, but the upper class members loved Apollos because he was elegant. He had the gift of eloquent speech, and, therefore, the members of the Corinth church began to do what we tend to do – attempt to mimic those who are more elegant or wealthy than we are, and, inevitably, compare ourselves and others to one another. They began to compare Apollos and Paul. Their comparison became unhealthy. In fact, a sign of an immature person – an immature church - and an immature Christian is when they begin to make unhealthy comparisons and engage in unhealthy competition, losing their focus entirely. In this case, they were so immature that they did not understand that Paul might have planted the seeds of their church and Apollos watered those seeds of growth, but it was always God who would provide the ultimate growth and development in the church and the congregation, in general. Further signs of an immature church, an immature ministry and / or an immature Christian is when they begin to compare - preachers with preachers, pastors with pastors, choirs with choirs, past servant leaders with present servant leaders, past deacons with present deacons, and past trustees with present trustees. It is a sign of Christian immaturity. It a sign that that person or congregation has placed their emphasis on man and not the God of the man that he sends. And, this is exactly what the Church at Corinth began to do.

One of the reasons the upper class members of this church loved Apollos was because they were impressed with his overt intellect and impressive wisdom that seemed to easily win over most people. He was a gifted speaker and, therefore, a popular and respected man. He was polished, and that fascinated people.

Now, Paul, a more humble man, intelligent but subtle, did not have the pizzazz and polish that this now misguided congregation appeared to respect. In fact, they began to think Paul was a fool, and they compared

in such circumstances. Everybody can be hurt and react inappropriately. Remember, people in pain have the tendency to hurt other people. So ... Paul sent the letter and waited for a response. Someone said "you are the master of your own words, but, once spoken or written, you become a slave to them". Thankfully, Paul, in waiting for the Corinth response, recognized there was hurt and pain on both sides (what the Bible identifies as "lupe", a Greek word), and so he was able to begin a healing process of sorts.

In looking at Paul's letter, he never mentioned the person who caused the pain in the first place because Paul was about pursuing reconciliation and restoration. However, in the harshness of the letter, it did cause the Corinth church to examine and repent for the pain they had caused. Also, the one who was the ringleader of the pain repented, which is, at times, quite a feat. There is always a ringleader of the pain. In our text, we are told that Paul sends another letter. It is called Paul's therapeutic letter, a letter of restoration. This letter focuses on how restoration can take place between two people who have hurt or offended each other intentionally or unintentionally. It is the kind of letter you write when "lupe", which means that mutual pain that we are discussing, has been caused by a friend, a brother, a preacher – anybody close enough to make an impact.

In this second letter, Paul extends an apology for causing or reacting to a pain in a negative way and Paul begins to move from focusing on the pain he caused to addressing the originator of his hurt. In this way, he is becoming productive and using the experience for good. All in all, Paul's letter was not to hurt the Corinth church. His motive, his reason for sending the letter is clear, as he states in Chapter 4 – "that they might know the love which he more abundantly has towards them." In other words, while he knows he was hurt in vengeance – he is approaching the offender in love.

The offender, Gaius, had taken a private matter and made it public. And, we know, in modern day, this happens often. People who want to hurt others will often do it publicly or loudly. In this way, it draws others into the web of pain and deceit. In Paul's case, the church community had been affected and infected by Gaius and his venom. In his response, Paul is not trying to cast blame at all, but he is acknowledging that the pain may have been meant for him, but ended up affecting the whole community, and that, as a result, absolute healing needed to begin right away.

In any situation, the community must not be involved in recycling or redistributing the pain; such participation would make anyone as guilty as the person who first began the cycle of hurt. Anytime we hear gossip and repeat it or give credence to any kind of exclusion, we are bullies too. We are not, in hushed tones, simply repeating what the bully did or said, we are participating in furthering that pain and damage. In fact, the big lesson we must learn at this point from Paul is what we do individually has corporate consequences because we are a community, a faith community, a family. We are not detached but, rather, are attached to each other. Yes, sometimes some things are an individual incident. Some things are just between two individuals and should be dealt with in that manner. But whenever it affects and infects the community, then the community has to be involved in the process of reconciliation. In fact, it affected the Corinth church in such a way that some people walked away from the church because they never thought Christians acted like that. Some people who were thinking about joining the church stayed away from the church. This, then, is an indication that the church at Corinth was not properly handling its hurt and became a stumbling block instead of a stepping-stone.

Paul, in this text, shows us how to handle "lupe" – or pain, when it has infected, disrupted, and negatively affected the community of faith. Let me say that the reason the community has to address it is because the person who might have caused the pain, the hurt, might not have known the magnitude of the pain, hurt, and harm that he or she had caused. It might have been an unintentional offense but there are innocent bystanders, and the person who starts it and those who perpetuate it must come to grips with the magnitude of the pain he or she has caused to the faith and non-faith community. Some people have been discouraged and affected by it to the point they have detached themselves from the church, becoming unbelievers who no longer want to be involved at all in a church. That, of course, is a very negative effect of what may have started as a small offense. We cannot let that happen – ever.

Instead, we need to learn from Paul and his letter of restoration. He tells us our responsibility, as the faith community, in verse 7. He says that we must forgive and comfort him (our offender), "lest perhaps he or she is swallowed up with over much sorrow". We'll come back to this in a bit, but for now put a pin right there and remember it: Paul said that it is the responsibility of the faith community to forgive and comfort the person who caused the pain. Paul explains to us how the faith community can go about and extend forgiveness, comfort, and restoration to that person. Paul also says that the first step must be taken by the one who caused the pain. Once the one you have hurt has reached out seeking forgiveness, you must begin the forgiveness process. Having been the recipient of pain, as well as the one who has caused pain, I sought healing myself, and that healing came from a seminar I attended in Lancaster, PA. It was at that session that I learned some principles that helped liberate me from the pain that I had personally and professionally experienced.

First and foremost, the person who caused the pain must acknowledge that pain – lupe – has been caused (2 Cor. 2: 5). Paul said, "if any caused grief, he hath not grieved me, but in part, that I may not over charge you all". Paul said the person grieved him, but that such pain was only a part of the greater offense – for they have hurt others too – you, me, the church to come. He cautions us, however, not to "overcharge" or tax them with the entire burden of pain and forgiveness, but, rather, to meet them halfway and to begin the process, as he did.

The reason the person who caused the pain has to acknowledge it is because you cannot comfort the misuse of power. The misuse of power – the disregarding of the feelings of others, the complete disregard that comes from intending to hurt someone, and the complete irresponsibility of unintentionally hurting someone – cannot be tolerated. The faith community must assist in the "justice" of the situation. Support does not go to the offender, but forgiveness and healing can be extended. Furthermore, the person who caused this cycle of pain must acknowledge it because there can be no therapy, healing, or restoration without justice.

Now – I asked you to keep this on your radar from earlier – Paul tells us that the person who caused the pain needs to be confronted in order to stop the cycle of hurt. And, while this is easy to understand, it is, however, often hard to execute – especially when it involves buy-in from the whole community. It is easier, in a way, if we can try to remember that those who cause pain often are victims of pain. Remember, "you cannot heal what you conceal". For example, if I have caused pain to someone in my congregation, and only that person and I know about it, then I have a

Christian obligation to go only to this person and acknowledge that I have caused pain – lupe. But if in my pain and anger to this person, I told everyone who would listen, then I must acknowledge my pain to not only the first person I hurt, but to everyone else I brought into the cycle because I did not just hurt harm one person anymore, I ended up hurting and harming others too. While this person in my congregation and I might have reconciled, those who were brought in on the peripheral are still living with the pain, and that is not right. Some things do require a corporate apology. For example, years ago, when President Bill Clinton had to address the Monica Lewinsky scandal, his apology address was to the whole nation - for although it was only he and she in the oval office, he brought us all in the situation.

This brings us to the second step in Paul's emotional therapy for the person who caused "lupe": Discipline or Punishment.

This point is not an easy one for Paul has said that, not only must the person acknowledge the pain he or she has caused, but also the church – the faith community – must distribute church discipline. And, of course, this is not easy. It is difficult to determine what is appropriate, and it is difficult to administer discipline to someone you may know, respect, or even pity. Human to human, deciding what to do in retribution that would help to move forward is problematic.

In Verse 6 Paul said, "Sufficient to such a man is this punishment, which was inflicted of many." Paul is telling us to be just and efficient with how we handle the offender. The community and the church must deal with sin or offense – and purge hurt. The church, in the spirit of Christ, must correct, confront, and rebuke offense and offenders. A law has been broken, and it needs to be handled less it weaken the community of faith.

In Paul's case, he calls upon the community to determine what the punishment – the discipline – should be. The offense was public so the discipline or punishment must be public to clearly communicate the healing that needs to happen as a result. Paul directs the community to absolutely use discipline but to be fair and discreet. After all, just as spoiled children get worse, so do adults, and just as children see lack of discipline as lack of love, so do adults. A discipline or an acknowledgement that a law has been broken shows the offender that the faith community does care. In fact, when we do not employ church discipline we are saying to that person, "You are not worthy or loved." For many of us, church discipline is a new concept because, for years, we have run wild in the church and the only person we disciplined was the pastor by voting him or her out. If we have applied church discipline in the past, we have done so for only those who committed certain acts like adultery or fornication, but we never discipline the person who has a nasty attitude or who has spoken about another or excluded someone, and those acts are sometimes worse than the archaic notion of punishable fornication, aren't they?

Many of us think we know what church discipline would entail, but do we really understand where it comes from and how it is handled? Most of us are in a faith communities where we do understand our boundaries and responsibilities. Do we always understand, however, when it is time for us and others to be accountable? I mean, it is difficult in everyday life to understand who is to "blame" in essence for work issues, family problems, or neighborhood grudges. In our church, where do we begin with such a notion? Most of us understand that there is give and take in a religious community; however, there are others who want the love and comfort, but they do not want the accountability – just like in a family. The church then has the potential to become a revolving door. We see people who come when they want to worship and feel love and leave when we question whether or not they stay faithful in worship, involved in some necessary discipleship, or an active part of the fellowship.

We must never forget that we serve a God who calls us to be responsible and accountable; therefore, the church is responsible to call each of its members into responsibility and accountability and to use the method of discipline to do so. The purpose of church discipline is not to destroy him or her – the member – but to lead him or her to Godly repentance. Church or Christian discipline is biblical and many of us do not like it or agree with it. It's the same at home. You may not like it, but it is needed. Discipline is a sign of love. God disciplines his children. The Bible said in the book of Hebrew that "the Lord disciplines, chastens those he loves" (Hebrews 12:6). God has given the church the gift of discipline and requires the church to carry out church discipline. What is discipline? The word "discipline" means teaching, training, correcting, rebuking, and punishment. There are laws that govern this country that if we break them and are caught, we will experience some form of punishment and penalty. It is also true in the faith community – God expects us to address and deal with offense. Discipleship is impossible without church discipline. Scripture teaches the responsibility of the church to discipline its members when necessary.

When the church extends Godly discipline, it means:
- I am my brother's keeper (Galatians 6:1).
- It demonstrates that none of us lives unto ourselves (Romans 14:8).
- It manifests the fact that a Christian life is a corporate life (I Corinthians 12:13, 23).

Just as in a natural family so in the spiritual family discipline is needed. It is needed to make order and happiness possible. Discipline guides the immature, stabilizes the weak, and causes people to come to maturity in the Lord. Discipline exercised in love gives individuals and congregation a sense of security, saves a backslider from hell, and prevents worse problems. Discipline is not simply for the pastor but for the members within the congregation.

The Bible talks about a two-fold purpose of church discipline: First for restoration (Gal. 6:1) and the second one is a discipline unto condemnation (I Corinthians 11:29-32) – and, we are not talking excommunication here – simply atoning for what you have done. In fact, in our text, Paul is referring to the first form of discipline. This discipline is not new; it is in the Old Testament as well as the New Testament. From Adam and Eve to Lot's wife, discipline was a part of God's law. In the New Testament, the Lord gives us a three-step process in regards to a brother or sister - or someone close to you - who offends you. We see this in Matthew 18:15-20. The Bible says you first must go to the person privately – go to him alone. This, as we've been discussing, involves going with the right attitude and manner or approach – the right words in the right spirit. Going alone, as I mentioned earlier, is the first foundational step. To bypass this step is to say you are not seeking reconciliation but segregation, and that is not acceptable.

The second step in understanding and applying what we call "Church Discipline" is if that person did not hear you, then you are to take two or three persons of faith with you to minister to that person his or her forgiveness, atonement, and, yes, discipline. To do this, you may need to involve some of his or her close friends or people in which he or she has confidence – hopefully, all of them spiritual and mature who have the gift of discernment. With this group of the faith community, we all need to understand that it would be our responsibility to shake he or she into reality and make him or her realize that something hurtful has been done.

The third step in the process of "Church Discipline" and admonition is to bring the person who refuses to repent and be reconciled before the church – the community. After all, once he or she has been made aware of the issue and confronted appropriately, the public display of forgiveness and restoration can begin. And, it may be daunting – frightening, but it is, as we mentioned earlier, a necessary step. When the whole congregation stands up and pleads with the person to be reconciled, hopefully he or she will listen and have a change of heart.

Now, if he or she did not hear the entire church, then the fourth step is, sadly, excommunication or distancing yourself from that person. This step is the last resort and only should be used when all else fails. And, finally, the fifth step is repentance and reconciliation.

The Bible tells us that if the person who caused the pain repents, then you have gained a brother or sister, but if he or she refuses, you have gained an enemy. And this does not just follow in the church community, but, rather, personally, we can follow these principles too.

Paul reminds us that if the person repents, then it is the responsibility of the faith community to forgive and comfort that brother or sister. Step number three: Forgive, comfort, and console.

The word "forgive" comes from two Greek words; it means to first let it go. The second meaning regarding the word "forgive" implies grace. Grace is God's riches at Christ's expense. It is unmerited favor. Grace is God giving you and me what we do not deserve, and mercy is God holding back what we do deserve. Paul said the faith community must extend to the person who caused the "lupe" repentance, forgiveness, and grace–unmerited favor. The word "comfort" is interesting here too – the

Greek word is "parakaleo", which means to come along side a person. Paul is saying that as we give the gift of forgiveness, we must call the person along side us or re-establish a horizontal, mutually beneficial, and friendly relationship. Walk alongside your offenders, as they walk alongside you. Remember the Bible said, "How can two walk together unless they agree?", even if that "agreement" is simply in forgiveness and forward motion in life.

For step four, Paul asks us to, "Reaffirm your love for them." (Verse 8)

"Reaffirm", in the Greek, means to formulate a resolution. To reaffirm your love to your offenders does not mean you like the act they have committed, but, rather, it means you resolve that you will not hate that person for committing it. We all know the modern saying, "Love the person; condemn the action." Basically, you may never find yourself liking that person, but you have to will yourself to love them. And, certainly, we've all been faced with those people. The person at work with whom we cannot get along, but we can sympathize when he or she goes through a divorce or the death of a loved one; we wish them goodwill, and we send our love their way. Love is truly an act of the will and, in that way, can work in these situations of forgiveness as well. We all can find the strength to love these who have hurt us. In that way, we can move on. Now, it is easier to hate than to love. And, many times, we can find 99 reasons to hate that person and can't find the very one reason to love him or her. Paul said that person needs the reaffirmation of the church. They need a resolution of respect. They need to be reassured of the community's love.

And, finally, we have the last step in Paul's plan. This step is not for the person who caused the pain, but, rather, it is for the church. This last step is not for the immature; it is not for the fair-weather friend of the church and of God. This step is one of the hardest. Paul says that the last step for both - the one who caused the pain and the faith community - is obedience. It is right there in Verse 9: "For to this end also did I write that I might know the proof of you whether you are obedient in all things" (2 Cor. 2:9). Paul said the evidence of your walk in the Lord is more than just Sunday morning; it is in your obedience. Now, when we think of obedience, we tend to look at it in light of our children. We want our children to be obedient, but we as adults don't like that word, "obedience", and we certainly don't think it applies to us. Paul said obedience is the proof of your faith, your walk. Obedience is the evidence of a mature saint. For many of us, that is hard because we don't like anyone, including God, to tell us what to do. We choose to come and go when we want. We choose to give when we feel like it, and God better not ask for even ten percent. We say we are raising a rebellious generation – a generation that does not respect authority and are lawbreakers. But may I say that the seed of rebellion that is in our children or grandchildren is in us.

Paul is not saying that you do not have an opinion, nor is Paul saying that what he's asking people to do is not painful and difficult – to forgive, to confront, to allow healing, to make it all public, and, above all, to execute, basically, blind obedience! But Paul is cautioning us to listen to God's authority and to be, quite simply, obedient. And.... we CAN do that.

Whether outside or inside the church, it is impossible to walk in disobedience and expect God to bless you. In these matters of hurt and forgiveness, His directives are so different. Disobedience does not produce blessings. Stories of disobedience and its consequences can be found throughout the Bible. In 2 Samuel 15:22-23, we find the story of Saul.

Saul says to Samuel, "I did do it but not the way God wanted it." And Samuel says to Saul, "Does the Lord delight in your burnt offering and the sacrifice or does He delight in you obeying His voice, His Word?" Samuel says, "Behold, to obey is better than sacrifice and to harken, to listen, than the fat of rams." Samuel then tells where disobedience comes from. He said a disobedient person is full with the spirit of rebellion. He said for rebellion is as the sin of witchcraft. Rebellion comes about because of arrogance. We think that we are higher than God and others and because of that mindset no servant leader, no deacon, and no pastor is going to call us into accountability for our lack of disobedience. But, for some of us, the issue to our disobedience is not rebellion but it is stubbornness. Samuel said, "Rebellion is as witchcraft and stubbornness is as idolatry". And some of us are not rebellious; we are wickedly stubborn. We are going to turn, but we are going to turn at our time and our pace. Their theme song is "I shall not be moved." This is why we are not further ahead in life, because we have a stubborn or a rebellious church. A certain generation of the children of Israel died in the wilderness because of their disobedience. And it's the little things that got them messed up. Samuel said to Saul, "Your disobedience is a sign that you have rejected God and his Word and thus he has rejected you" (2 Samuel 15:23).

In closing, Paul says, in 2 Corinthians, that the evidence of our spiritual walk or salvation is not how great we sing, not how great we shout, not how great we preach and usher and collect the offering, but it's in our obedience in all things – meaning the big things and even the little things. Paul says "so if you are obedient even when we don't feel like it and extend forgiveness to that person, I, too, forgive". He says but the longer you function in disobedience "in all or anything", we have given place to Satan – the demonic – we have given Satan an advantage, which means we become at a disadvantage, when it should be that we are at an advantage and Satan at a disadvantage.

Trust and obey for there is no other way to be happy in Jesus than to trust and obey.

To Walk, Teach, Learn and Live in Forgiveness
An Epilogue to Unit Three

Your directives, readers, after this long and difficult unit, are simple. Think of one time you offended someone. Think of how you felt – how they felt – why you did what you did – and how you feel now. Write a letter to that person, telling them how you would like to see the situation resolve – how you would like them to think of you – and how both lives should move forward.

_____

_____

_____

_____

_____

Now, dear readers, think of a time during which you were hurt or offended. Think about your pain – what you did – how you felt – and if you vowed revenge or retribution. Think about the person who caused that pain and whether or not you can see that he or she is hurting – has been wounded – or is acting out. Think about how you would handle that situation – that forgiveness – now. Write that person your letter here:

_____

_____

_____

_____

_____

_____

_____

_____

_____

UNSHACKLED FROM BROKENNESS:

LEARNING TO LIVE AGAIN

2 CORINTHIANS 7:10

Sometimes it is difficult to figure out what God's purpose and plan for our lives truly might be. Often, when we explore, as we have been doing, what it feels like to gain freedom from all of our emotional bondage and all of our selfish, insecure, and fearful beliefs, we begin to see a little more clearly what we need to do – for ourselves, for others, and for God. And the prerequisite for this type of improvement or increase in all aspects of our lives is becoming unshackled. We have to become unshackled from all the weights in life that hinder us and create stagnation in our lives. We can't grow if we don't let go of hatred, jealously, self-doubt, prejudice, and other heavily negative and damaging qualities in our lives. To use a Bible analogy, we cannot live in Canaan, the Promised Land, with the mentality that the Egyptians had. In other words, we cannot celebrate God's best while we are behaving or creating a mindset for ourselves that puts us at our worst.

> *Sometimes it is difficult to figure out what*
> *God's purpose and plan for our lives truly might be.*

Remember when we examined being "Unshackled from Un-forgiveness." You may recall we approached the idea non-traditionally, focusing on forgiving the person who may have caused us or someone else pain in the first place rather than focusing on what we commonly think of as the "victims". We discussed the fact that the person who caused the pain probably had experienced pain at one time in his or her life. Further, often, in shame, the person who caused pain will not reach out. For these reasons, those around the person, including his or her victims, need to reach out and forgive. Within this circle of forgiveness, the person who caused the pain will be called by the faith community to acknowledge the pain that he or she has caused. As a result, bad feelings don't fester, the person feeling and / or causing pain is embraced, once again, by the church, and the person or people who feel victimized by pain are redeemed and healed. It is important to note that as these people acknowledge what they've done, the faith community must reaffirm their love to them, comfort them, console them, and, yes, forgive them. The greatest gift we can give someone who has caused this odd, unintentional, and ongoing loop of pain is forgiveness; it is also the best gift we can give ourselves.

Now, on that note, let's really consider the pain these people have caused. Let's forget about why it was caused and let's try to focus on healing and moving from any bad feelings. Sometimes, this feat is hardest for that victim we mentioned earlier – that person who has experienced pain possibly had to relive some of it as the perpetrator was made to acknowledge what he or she has done and attempted to pick up and move forward, often times sad, hurt, defeated, and broken. It is that person we focus on now.

Paul, the apostle of our Lord Jesus Christ, gives us a theology of pain and a theology of those who suffer wrongfulness at the hands of others. There are four emotions related to this cycle with which we are all familiar: desire, pleasure, fear, and pain. Of course we know that desire and pleasure are positive, but fear and pain are negative. And whether we like it or not, in this life, we not only experience desire and pleasure, but also fear and pain – and on a regular basis.

Pain is a strong feeling. You recall from earlier in the book that Paul and the Corinthian church had both experienced pain. The Corinthian church was questing and challenging Paul's apostolic authority, and they were seeking to accuse Paul of embezzlement or actually stealing of money. Paul was wounded because they questioned his good faith message and motive, but he was wounded further because of the person who started the rumor or the gossip. It came from an unexpected source, one of Paul's close friends. And, in fact, don't we often find that it is the person who is the closest to us who can create the greatest pain in us.

As a result of all this pain, Paul leaves the Corinthian church wounded and sends them a letter that he writes with tears and with pain. As a result of this exchange, the Corinthian church sees the light, Paul sees his wrongful doing in over-reacting and becoming angry about the situation, and they all begin this process of moving from brokenness to wholeness. Restoration and reconciliation began to take place. Remember all parties – the one who causes the pain and the one who receives it – should both always be considered the victims.

As a result of this communication, Paul begins to interact once again with the Corinthian church as a faith community, dealing both with the person who caused the pain as well as with those who received it. It may have been difficult – there were pain and tears, but Paul wanted to focus on the people, including himself and his friend, who experienced brokenness, and begin the process of healing and, most importantly, a restoration to wholeness. And truly, in everyday life, how difficult is it to tell someone that God wants us all to be whole? In order for all of us to become whole, despite pain and hurt and alienation at times, we must come to grips with the pain in our lives. Remember, God cannot heal what we conceal. Reveal to heal. This should be a way of life for all of us – a renewed feeling / philosophy that we repeat again and again.

In 2 Corinthians, the church at Corinth repents for causing pain. At the beginning of the chapter seven, Paul shares with them that, while pain, lupe, or brokenness had been caused to him as well as to them by a number of people in the church close to everyone – even friends – it did not change his affection or commitment to them and nor should it change theirs to him. Paul vows to continue boasting to everyone about the church's faith, and they, in turn, forever consider him the father of their church. Even in the midst of Paul's troubles – from all sides – conflicts on the inside and fear on the outside – he was comforted by his relationship with God. God absolutely comforts the downcast, and this we must all remember. Paul had Titus – that friend who really never wronged him despite perception, and we all need a friend like that – someone of the faith who will not judge us nor condemn us but will bring comfort to us. Titus' name means a nurse. Nurses are people who are supposed to be filled with compassion and empathy – not just sympathy. We all need a Titus in our life to help nurse us from brokenness to wholeness. For the reality is we cannot do it by ourselves. Titus can be a family member, a friend, or a close friend who will walk with us through the most painful times and situations. I thank God that I have several Tituses in my life. Some of them are ministers of the Gospel and most of them are not, but they showed up and continue to show up at the right time to nurse me from brokenness to wholeness, and I will be eternally grateful.

Paul, in 2 Corinthians chapter seven, shows us three primary things for preaching and teaching on healing from pain. We see his motive, his method, and, finally, his message.

Paul's Motive

Paul said for even if he had caused them pain, his motive for the pain was not to hurt them but to help them. Paul said the letter that he wrote to them did not just hurt them but hurt him. And yet, he had not relished his pastoral duty to discipline them – he was writing to call them into repentance. He wanted them to know that while he was not happy over the brokenness or pain that they experienced, he did rejoice that the pain led them to sorrow, which called them to repentance. He wanted them to know that there is a pain that leads to total brokenness – woundedness – and there is a pain that leads to healing. The pain that leads to brokenness and death is a pain that God is not involved in, but there is a "lupe" in which God is involved and it leads to a change of heart, repentance, and a change of mind that leads to salvation." That word, salvation, by the way, means health, wellness, and wholeness. Paul said the pain of this world, the lupe of this world, will lead to regret and death, but the lupe that God is involved in makes you and I not bitter, but better – not a mess, but a miracle. The Corinthian church exemplified repentance.

Thus, Paul walks with the Corinthian church through the pain that leads to life, health, and wholeness. When we examine the biblical text, we see that Paul gives us seven steps to wholeness. While it matters to Paul and the Lord what the brokenness is and who caused the pain, the Lord is more concerned about the cure of the soul. The emphasis, at this point, in Paul's life is not on the pain or brokenness, but it is on how we heal and become unshackled from the brokenness, the lupe, the pain. How do we make sure that the pain – the lupe – the brokenness does not become president – ruler – of our lives? Paul invites us to take a journey with him, similar to his journey with the church at Corinth – a journey from brokenness to wholeness.

The Corinthians' genuine sorrow over the pain they caused produced several things. Those things that Godly sorrows produce were the steps to their healing. There are seven distinct things that were produced, which moved them from brokenness to wholeness. Of course, as students of the Bible, we understand that seven is the number of completion. God wants us to be completely healed from the wounds – the brokenness. He wants us to be healed in the words of David Evans of David Evans Ministries, "Healed Without Scars". This is not partial healing, but complete healing.

Let me say that these steps are for the brokenhearted and those who want to walk in complete wholeness and not brokenness. These steps are for those who will no longer use the pain of their past or present as an excuse for not becoming all that God intends and wants them to be. Jesus said in the Gospel of Luke 4:18, "The spirit of the Lord is upon him to preach the Gospel to the poor; he has sent me to heal the brokenhearted, to proclaim liberty to the captives, to set at liberty those who are oppressed."

Healing from brokenness is available to whose who are willing to take these steps and apply them to their life and let the healing power of the Holy Spirit begin to heal your broken heart.

Paul said, in 2 Corinthians 7:9 that the steps he is about to lay out are a Godly way of dealing with pain. In other words, there is a positive, Godly way of dealing with brokenness, hurt, and pain, and then there is a negative, ungodly way of addressing the pain. Someone said hurting people, hurt people, and healthy people, help people. You can't help someone if you are harboring anger, rage, bitterness, or malice towards him or her. There is a Godly and ungodly manner of dealing with lupe, with brokenness, with wounds.

Many of us ignore and refuse to recognize that we have been hurt. Many of us deal with pain by building a wall around ourselves to keep people out and the wall has kept us in. Many of us who have experienced pain turn around and cause pain. My brothers and sisters in Christ and Creation, God has prescribed for you and me a Godly manner to handling brokenness, pain, lupe. That word, "pain", carries the meaning of frustration, physical and mental distress, depression, and deep woundedness – burning. Paul said Godly sorrow produces these things. In fact, he said that Godly sorrow produces repentance: a change of mind and a change of heart – turning around. He wants us to understand that there is a difference in being sorry or sorrowful and being Godly sorrowful. You see, when you are Godly sorrowful for what you have done, it will bring about a change of mind and a change of heart that will bring about a change of action. If there is no change of mind and heart then there will be no change of action. Paul said this sorrow that is Godly leads to repentance but it ends up as salvation – wholeness, wellness. But the pathway from brokenness to wholeness is repentance – a change of heart and mind, which begins with Godly sorrow.

Paul's Godly Manner / Method: Seven Steps to Wholeness

The first step on this journey to wholeness is meaning – let's expound on this. I mean, we all know what assigning meaning to anything does, but this is different. You see, genuine sorrow produces these seven things – a phenomenon of feeling, if you will, in a person who is seeking to be made whole. Paul said that when you are Godly sorrowful for what happened to you and what happened to others, these steps will be evident and … productive, according to Dr. Laurence Wellborn, Professor at the United Theological Seminary in Trotwood, Ohio at a session delivered recently in Lancaster, Pennsylvania.

Godly sorrow, first, produces earnestness or a concerted effort to make amends. The key word in that sentence is "earnestness". Earnestness carries the meaning of diligence, forwardness, haste, striving, to give all that you can in casting yourself (and others) forward. Do you want to be whole? Every time in the Gospel before Jesus heals a person, he asks them, "Do you want to be made whole?" Some of us have been down and broken for so long that getting up is not even on our mind. No one can have the earnestness for you. You have to get it yourself. You are the only one who can drink the healing water. I can take you to the water, but I cannot force you to drink.

The second step on this journey to wholeness is what Paul calls an apologia, or apology, and with it, comes defensiveness. This is truly an eagerness to vindicate oneself. When we apologize, we are seeking to clear ourselves. It means you want to give an explanation of why we acted the way we did. I acted that way because you acted that way. It was once said that, life consists of five percent of what happens to you and 95 percent of how we react to it. We cannot control people's attitude; all we can control is our own attitude when we respond to anything done to us. You cannot control what people say about you. People are going to always talk. Even when you are doing something positive, people are going to talk. Jesus did say, "Offense will come." You can't do anything about that. What you can control is how much you are going to let what people say about you affect you and change you. You have to remain true to who you are. What we tend to do is become defensive. We want to give a reason – an explanation.

And how many of you know even when you give an explanation it is never good enough to stop people from talking. Paul never defended his apostolic authority nor gave a defense for requiring what he did from the church at Corinth. Remember that when you are right, the Lord will fight your battles. Some battles you don't have to fight because the battle is not yours; it's the Lord's. Step two is when we are seeking to clear ourselves – to make sorrow, to affect with sadness – a verbal defense, an argument, a clearing of one's self.

The third thing that Godly sorrow produces was what Paul calls "indignation – vexation – irritation". The Corinthian's church had indignation against Paul's opponent. This brings with it a feeling that it ought not been this way. It ought not to have happened and not to me. Anger is present on this step. Many of us don't get angry, and then when we do get angry, we get angry over the wrong stuff. And if you are not careful, anger can turn into rage. Remember anger is not bad, but rage is. Remember, I control anger – you control anger – but rage controls you. We established this earlier. Now this is the step that many of us get stuck on. We are angry with the person, we are mad with the church, and we get mad or angry with the whole world. This is why people leave the church for a season or eventually leave for good.

Fourth, is what Paul calls, fear or alarm at their own passivity and its injurious affects. This is the stage when the person wants to draw back. He or she does not want to move forward because they have built identities around the pain, the wound, the brokenness. The fear of the unknown, the fear of what people would think – self-imposed fear. The fear of being on their own. The fear of starting over. The fear of failure. At this stage, the person cannot conceive or perceive life without the pain, the lupe, the brokenness, because they no longer posses the pain but the pain now possesses them.

Fifth, is vehement desire – this word carries the meaning of longing. At this stage, this person has a longing to be made whole, to get well, and to move from brokenness to wholeness. It's the longing that calls for action. I recall a story in the Bible about a woman who had an "issue of blood", or just an issue for twelve long years. She longed to be healed. She spent all her money and grew worse. She was ceremonially and culturally unclean, but between her condition and the culture, Christ came, and she said within herself, "If I can touch the hem of his garment I know I will be made whole or well" (Mark 5:28). She had a desire – a longing to be well, to be made whole, and to be healed. The woman wanted to be made whole so badly that she pressed past the pain to get to Jesus. You see, until you want it badly enough, you are not going to do anything about it. For some of us, we play around with being made whole, but it is not a longing, burning desire, because if it were, we would get the necessary help that we need. We would do whatever was prescribed for us. What we want is the absence of pain, but not real wholeness. We want the pain to simply stop.

The sixth is Zeal. The Greek word is "Zelos", which means fire – a burning, an excitement of mind. It is connected with hope, it is the "fervor of spirit" – something, for which we all strive. Of course, we are all born with a tremendous spirit; it is these moments of pain that knock the wind out of our sails and leave us lacking in this once inherent sense of self, spirit – God and beyond – OUR own feeling to God and others. We need to work to get this back.

Finally, the seventh is vindication, which is, basically, justice – punishment – a readiness to see justice done. That word carries the meaning of righting the wrong, the balance. You, as the person who has been broken or has experienced pain, have a responsibility to right the wrong, or right the balance. In all of this this person can prove that they are innocent by virtue of his or her repentance, as we've established. Yes, we have all sinned, but to sin and wrong another by failing to do right requires absolute repentance – and willing repentance – is in order.

Paul's Message

Paul shared with them the purpose, or motive, for his writing. It is as if he was telling them that he wrote for the sake of the one who suffered the wrong, who experienced the pain, the lupe, and the hurt. Paul says that the reason he addresses healing from un-forgiveness and brokenness – the whole motive for preaching to both the person who caused the wrong and the person who received the wrong – is to show that it matters not which side you fall on; the purpose for the preaching and teaching is so you can see how much God cares for you.

When you see the sign that someone cares for you, you listen – you take notice – you act and react. Remember, it is not when they avoid or overlook your pain, faults, or shortcomings, it's when they see the pain, the faults, the shortcomings and help you with them or accept them. We all sing songs in our churches weekly that say that "God looks beyond our faults and sees our needs"; however, those songs are actually theologically incorrect. Our God who cares does not look beyond our faults, He accepts them; He helps us learn from them. If He did overlook it all, then there would be no need for Jesus, for Jesus came because God saw our faults. God saw our faults and delivered this good news: I don't just see your faults; I see your needs. And sure, we do feel that our needs are for cars or houses or jobs, but those are wants. Our needs stem from being whole and wanting to be continually healed. This is why God sent the great physician – to heal our sin-sick souls. And now, I want you to look, examine, and remember the method, the motive, and the message as I've detailed for you here.

Beyond changes in yourself,
what would you like to see happen in your life?

The message is that God cares about me enough that He sent his Word to heal my brokenness.

To Find Yourself Again: An Epilogue to Unit Four

I have to tell you here – as I can almost see you all nodding knowingly, thinking you understand easily what it means to heal from brokenness – to forgive – to move on. Please note, before you begin your journey of restoration, that you need to take stock of how you may have been changed by this movement, however. How did being hurt change you? How do you want to change moving forward? What changed that should be made the same again?

Beyond changes in yourself, what would you like to see happen in your life? What would you like to help others achieve? Do you want to go back to school? Do you want to work with the homeless and help them achieve some happiness? These appear to be easy questions to ask, but…. as we all know, they are harder to execute. It is truly difficult, at times, to move a big change forward or to elicit change in another.

Make your peace with your past. Put your mindset in the here and now. And... list four succinct things you would like to achieve in the next year on the next page. Be sure to include one personal item, one community-related item, one item related to a past friend or someone you may have misjudged, and one item devoted to a greater good for your church or the world – a contribution, a change of heart, or a promise. Then.... make it all happen. God knows you can do it, I know you can do it, and YOU know you can do it (Phil. 4:13).

_____

_____

_____

_____

_____

_____

_____

_____

_____

_____

_____

_____

_____

_____

_____

_____

CLOSING NOTES

I have taken you, my readers, on quite a journey, and I would understand if you needed time to digest all that I've presented to you. To help you in this last part of the process – that process to learn to dance with broken bones – I want to reiterate a few points, explain your role in all of this a bit more, and send you confidently on your way, having become better for reading this book.

We have learned many things about pain, forgiveness on all levels, and moving forward. I say "forgiveness on all levels" because we need to forgive ourselves for past behaviors first. We need to understand that we are not bad people because of a failed marriage, a broken promise, or a failed career. We also need to stop pigeon-holing ourselves – seeing ourselves as the divorced single mother ONLY; or "the guy who got fired"; or, simply, as a bad friend or son or daughter. We have to pick up, face our issues, and make them right, whether that is making amends for what we've done – dusting ourselves off and trying a new career – or simply telling ourselves and, therefore, the world, that it is OK to have failed once; it is OK to survive a bad marriage; it is OK to have stolen and been sorry for it; it is OK to have forgotten our roles as parents or children only to return better and more attentive than before; and it is OK to rejoin the faith community.

On a similar note, we have to see our faith community, our neighborhood, our families, as flawed but wonderful places into which all are welcome – including people who have "wronged" us and others. We need to make sure to hold people accountable, and not in a petty way, but in a way that helps others see where they need to change or improve and rejoin the world renewed and restored.

All of us are individuals – beautiful, imperfect, flawed, wonderful, seeking, helping, loving individuals. We deserve to see ourselves as God does. We deserve to live our lives and all that entails. And, certainly, life will send us challenges – illness, war, bad days and good days – and, having danced with joy and without restraint, our dance with broken bones, we will be prepared for all that it has to offer.

See you on the Dance Floor.

Dr. Jasmin W. Sculark, known as "Dr. Jazz", is a native of the Island of Trinidad and Tobago. She accepted the Lord Jesus Christ into her life at a very early age, and shortly thereafter, she accepted God's calling and went into full time ministry.

An accomplished pastor, teacher, and preacher, Dr. Sculark, or "Dr. Jazz", is a proven trailblazer of "firsts" for her congregation at Shiloh Baptist Church in York, PA and in her community, in general. She is noted for being the first female to be called to pastor a Baptist church in York, PA entirely, and has secured herself a place in the community as a progressive ministry visionary by being the first to ordain women as Deacons at Shiloh. As a lifelong proponent of all people striving to better themselves, she formed the Empowerment Community Development Corporation in 2003, a ministry vehicle that provides computer-training classes for seniors and teens in partnership with the Capital City Project as well as an after school tutoring program and summer program called "SMART Kids for Christ".

In addition to her outreach programs, Dr. Jazz is focused on improvement and expansion in her community and in July of 2007, she and her Shiloh congregation purchased a new sanctuary for the church with multiple classrooms, which was valued at two million dollars. The new sanctuary/ building was dedicated in September 2009. Under her spiritual leadership and teaching, Shiloh has welcomed over 2000 plus new believers, and she has added and developed over 40 new ministries to meet the needs of her church and community.

A sought after preacher both nationally and abroad, Dr. Jazz's preaching invitations include: Shaw University, Howard University's School of Divinity, and Hampton Ministers' Conference. She has preached in Nigeria, St. Croix, her own Native Island Trinidad and Tobago, West Africa, and at the Millennium Pastors and Laypersons' Conference in the Bahamas, to name just a few. Her sermon "Don't Worry, Be Happy" was featured in the African-American Pulpit Judson Press Publication who also nominated her as one of the "20 Young Preachers to watch in the

New Millennium". Dr. Jazz received the Gardner C. Taylor Distinguished Preaching Award 2010 and is also featured in the Gardner C. Taylor Distinguished Preaching Series.

Dr. Jazz received her license to preach the Gospel on February 4, 1992 at the Mt. Pleasant Baptist Church in Washington, DC and was ordained in July 1999 at the Mt. Olivet Baptist Church in Columbus, Ohio. She is currently the Senior Pastor of the Shiloh Baptist Church in York, PA and Founder and President of The Daughter of Thunder Ministries. A graduate of the Practical Bible College in Vestal, NY and Washington Bible College in Lanham, MD, she received her Masters in Theological Studies from the Trinity Lutheran Seminary in Columbus, OH, and in December of 2007, she received her Doctor of Ministry Degree from the United Theological Seminary in Dayton, Ohio. Her greatest desire is to be found faithful in the task God has given her. This is her first book.